WRITE IT
LEVEL IT
TEACH IT

WRITE IT LEVEL IT TEACH IT

Save time and boost learning with your own model texts

MATT BEIGHTON

CORWIN

A SAGE company
2455 Teller Road
Thousand Oaks, California 91320
(0800)233-9936
www.corwin.com

SAGE Publications Ltd
1 Oliver's Yard
55 City Road
London EC1Y 1SP

SAGE Publications India Pvt Ltd
B 1/I 1 Mohan Cooperative Industrial Area
Mathura Road
New Delhi 110 044

SAGE Publications Asia-Pacific Pte Ltd
3 Church Street
#10-04 Samsung Hub
Singapore 049483

Editor: Amy Thornton
Senior project editor: Chris Marke
Cover design: Wendy Scott
Typeset by: C&M Digitals (P) Ltd, Chennai, India
Printed in the UK

Library of Congress Control Number: 2022933350

British Library Cataloguing in Publication Data

A catalogue record for this book is available from the
British Library.

ISBN 978-1-5297-8154-0
ISBN 978-1-5297-8153-3 (pbk)

At SAGE we take sustainability seriously. Most of our products are printed in the UK using responsibly sourced
papers and boards. When we print overseas we ensure sustainable papers are used as measured by the
PREPS grading system. We undertake an annual audit to monitor our sustainability.

CONTENTS

ACKNOWLEDGEMENTS

I don't like writing acknowledgements because I'm terrified that I'll miss somebody vitally important. However, there are some people without whom this book wouldn't have been, or at least would have been a very poor imitation of what it is.

I need to start by thanking Amy and Sarah at SAGE/Corwyn. Without Amy's belief in this book and her faith in the fact that I knew what I was talking about, it wouldn't be here at all. Without Sarah driving me forward, making sure that I wrote what needed to be written and that it all made sense, it would probably be a lot of waffle delivered months late. You both made the process easier at every step of the way, so thank you.

To Margaret at Renaissance®, I owe a debt of gratitude for returning my call and opening my eyes even further to how the whole process of levelling texts works. Your passion and enthusiasm is infectious and renewed my energy levels at key moments in the process. Thank you, Margaret, and to everyone else at Renaissance who shared their research with me.

I will be forever indebted to Rob at The Literacy Shed for taking a chance and changing the direction of my life. Without his belief and support, I would never have taken the leap to writing full time and wouldn't have had the experience or confidence to write this book. Thank you, I owe you!

Beyond that, I need to thank some of my oldest colleagues and friends. Amy, for being an awesome sister and teaching inspiration. Polly, the great detective, for holding each other up in the beginning and making me laugh. Donna, for your endless patience and showing me how it's all done. Josh for the help and drinks along the way. And Lindsay for everything we've been through, from your support and understanding to your friendship, chocolate and laughs. But also to all of them for their feedback and notes before I delivered that initial session to hundreds of teachers. I still owe you all a pizza; I haven't forgotten!

As with everybody who achieves anything, I couldn't have done it without the love and support of my family. Amy and Rebecca, you are a constant source of amusement. Mum and Dad, your unfaltering belief is why I am who I am. Most important of all, I owe so much to my wife, Toni. Her continued strength and support, and her willingness to step into the breach when I'm out and about living my dream can never be repaid. Thank you most of all for being there and believing in me.

ABOUT THE AUTHOR

Matt Beighton spent nearly nine years as a primary school teacher before leaving at the beginning of 2020 to write full-time. At the same time as teaching, Matt began to write for children and has so far published eight children's books. He also creates reading comprehension content for *The Literacy Shed*.

It is this combined experience that gives Matt the know-how to create this book. It draws on his experience as a teacher, author and content creator to provide useful and useable information that will help teachers to save time and increase the effectiveness of their own content.

As well as writing books, Matt travels the country inspiring the next generation of writers by running writing workshops with schools. These exciting events vary from exercises in creating characters and plot, through using the idea of branching narratives to explore story structure all the way to his new and popular *Fightin' Writin'* Workshops, which engage even the most reluctant writers.

If you'd like to find out more about Matt's work, join his newsletter or just get in touch with him, you can find him at:

https://mattbeighton.co.uk/
info@mattbeighton.co.uk
Twitter@mattbeighton

FOREWORD

BY ROB SMITH

Imagine being asked to write about something that you are not an expert in. You will need to write it in an unfamiliar style and use techniques that you have had very little experience with. That sounds like a tough task, yet we ask many children to do this regularly. We understand that this is a difficult task for many children and so we provide them with scaffolds and models to support them over this knowledge and skills gap.

I have been teaching for almost two decades and it was not until recently that I began to think about the effect of having a model too simple or too difficult upon which many children depend. It was Matt Beighton who showed me some simple techniques that can be utilised easily to create texts that are at a suitable level for the children in our classes.

It may be true that children are able to emulate some of the features or the language used in a more complex or advanced text, but often it will be simple mimicry rather than a deeper understanding of the skills.

What Matt successfully shows is how important and also how easy it is to create content for your classroom, which will be appropriately pitched at the reading ability of the children. The children's ability to access and use examples of text supplied by the teacher is pivotal in their ability to achieve success within their own writing, and Matt clearly explains why this is and what can happen to a child's writing when the balance is not right.

His straightforward, structured style ensures that his methods and explanations are simple to follow. It also enables the teacher to dip in and out and adapt their teaching and resources, rather than the need to adopt an entirely new whole-school approach.

Matt's book allows the teacher to achieve success within an area of teaching, which is often the most time consuming and, for some, the most challenging. At a time when the workload for teachers seems to be getting heavier, this book is an ideal way to make planning and resourcing lessons so much more effective for the students and easier for the teacher.

Rob Smith is the creator and curator of the award-winning website *The Literacy Shed* and author of *Shedwords*. After a 12-year career as a primary teacher, Rob now delivers writing workshops to students and professional development for teachers across the UK and around the world. Follow @LiteracyShed on Twitter and Instagram and search for the #ShedWords hashtag to find out more.

INTRODUCTION: ABOUT THIS BOOK

Hello, welcome and thank you for coming along with me on this adventure. If you've picked up this book, then we already share a passion for teaching reading and writing. I hope that you will find something different within these pages that will not only enthuse, but also help you to reduce the time it takes you to create content for your class, while also making it more effective at the same time. It sounds like a tall order, but it can definitely be done.

This isn't a book that will tell you how to teach reading and writing within your classroom. There are lots of books out there that do a great job of this. Instead, this book is all about you and how you create content for your class. There is information in here that will be useful for English curriculum leads either within a school or across a family of schools, but it will all be useful to you as a classroom teacher.

While most of the examples and content lean towards primary education, that's mainly because that is my area of experience. The same processes and ideas will work just as well in a secondary environment.

I suppose this would be a good time to introduce myself and why and how this book came about. I've had a varied career path, winding through web development and marketing before eventually settling down as a primary school teacher when my first daughter was born. For almost a decade, I've plied my trade and hopefully had an impact, however small, on hundreds of children's lives.

During my last few years of teaching, I began to write children's books. That started as a way of showing the children in my class that you *could*, in fact, write a book using all the grammar objectives that I was teaching them (it turns out that you can't, or at least not a very good book). Once I'd started, there was no stopping the writing train.

While I was doing that, I had the opportunity to start writing reading comprehensions for The Literacy Shed. Since then, I've written over 1,000 short texts, all of which have been levelled at using the systems described in Part 2 of this book – that's over half a million words and counting.

Around about the same time, the school I was teaching in moved to a writing framework that required us to write a lot more of our own content. For me, that was fine. I was writing my own books, writing for The Literacy Shed and it was easy enough to write short texts for my class.

It was at this point that I realised that we'd never assessed the reading level of any of the content we'd created previously. I asked around in different schools and nobody was doing it there either. Until I started to write and level the texts for The Literacy Shed, it had never even occurred to me that this might a thing we would be able to do.

Not only that, I realised that a lot of teachers across various schools struggled to create their own content. Some were taking far more time than is reasonable, some struggled with ideas and some were creating content that didn't have a clear purpose or structure.

This wasn't their fault. A lot of training is available that shows teachers how to structure lessons to teach writing or how to use various modelling frameworks, but there isn't anything that I could find that actually helped teachers to write their own content in an effective and efficient way.

By then, my writing career was taking up more of my time as was teaching (when doesn't it?) and it became clear that I had to make a choice. So, at Christmas 2019, after nearly a decade, I left teaching and became a full-time writer. Then, the pandemic hit.

I decided to try to put together a workshop that I could deliver to teachers to help them with the things I thought were missing from the training that I'd had, that would help them to create content effectively and efficiently. I delivered that workshop online to roughly 300 teachers and their feedback showed me that there really was a need for more of it.

That workshop and my own experiences as a teacher and a writer eventually led me to this book. Every activity and suggestion is something that I have used either as a teacher or when writing my own books or content for The Literacy Shed.

Over three parts, I will go into detail about why it is so important to at least be aware of the reading level of your content, how to assess and alter it to make sure it is doing the job you need it to, and finally how to create content quickly, easily and that will have the maximum impact in your class or school.

When you handed over your money and bought this book, you may have noticed that you didn't sign a contract. You are under no obligation to use every single idea in the book nor to use them in the way I've prescribed them. One of the things that used to frustrate me whenever I had training as a teacher was somebody telling me how to do something and that it was the only or best way to do it. I promise I won't do that to you.

All of the ideas, suggestions and recommendations in this book are useful (I suppose I would say that), but you need to see which ones will work in your own context and take them and adapt them. Make them your own and, if you do, let me know how you've used them and the impact they've had. You can drop me an email at info@mattbeighton.co.uk or via Twitter @mattbeighton.

Whether you read the book cover to cover or drop in and out of parts is also entirely up to you. It has been written in a way that any important information that you may need from another chapter is referenced, so you should be able to find what you need. I hope that everyone will read Part 1, because I whole-heartedly believe that making sure your content is at a suitable reading level is critical within the classroom.

When I looked back and thought about the pieces of content that my classes struggled with, I took them and ran them through the analysers in Part 2. Every single one of them was either too high or way too low. I can't help but think about how much easier those lessons would have been for me as a teacher, and how much more accessible to my class, had I known about and levelled them correctly.

Wherever you are in your career, I hope you approach the concepts within these pages with an open mind and take something away that will reduce your workload and make teaching your class that little bit easier.

PART 1

WRITE IT: WHAT ARE MODEL TEXTS AND WHERE MIGHT YOU USE THEM?

1

OPPORTUNITIES TO CREATE CONTENT

THE MOST INFLUENTIAL AUTHOR IN YOUR CLASSROOM

It's probably easiest to begin this part of the book with a really important question: who is the most influential author in your classroom? You might even ask your pupils this question and see what they say. You might be able to come up with a list of authors who you think have an influence on the attitudes or writing styles of those lucky enough to be in your class, but I would argue that you are wrong if you think they are the most influential. So, then, who is the most influential? You are. You may not consider yourself an author or that the texts you create for your class have any influence, but you are and they do. Hear me out. When I first had the idea for this book, I sent out a questionnaire to a little over a hundred teachers and asked them a few questions about model texts in their classrooms. Over 55 per cent said that they had to write a model text or something similar at least once a fortnight. If each of those texts is roughly 500 words, that's nearly 10,000 words of highly tailored content specifically created for your class. If you're doing that once a week, as nearly 30 per cent of teachers are, that's 20,000 words.

Some of your pupils may say that they prefer to read more famous authors, but your content is far more impactful – or at least it has the potential to be. Even if you don't consider yourself an author, the children in your class might without either of you knowing it. Try giving them one of your texts but don't tell them who wrote it. Ask them what they thought of it and you might be surprised by how they respond. They will certainly treat it the same as if it were written by a 'professional' writer. You have the potential to tap into that interest and to use it to improve the outcomes in your class. This book is designed to help you step up your writing game and help you to reach that potential.

Those teachers who were responding to my survey were only considering what most of us refer to as 'model texts'. You might know them as WAGOLLs, shared texts, example texts or something else – basically, they are texts that you create as model examples for your pupils to read, dissect and then emulate in their own work.

However, those texts aren't the only times that teachers create content for their own classroom; if they were, the job would be easier and planning would take a lot less time. Many teachers create their own reading comprehension texts or spend time writing interesting and fact-filled information sheets for their class to use during history, geography or science lessons. What about word problems during a maths lesson? All of these are written by you, specifically for the children in your class. They all build up to rather a large number of words written and tailored to the 30 children sitting in front of you each day. If that doesn't make you an influential author, then I don't know what does!

TEACHER TASK 1

Let's take a break and spend some time thinking about what I've just said. Look at your timetable and planning for an average week in your class. Get out all the content that you put in front of your pupils and lay it out on a table. This should be for every single lesson: maths, PE, French, English, history, etc. It doesn't matter if you created it yourself or if you downloaded it from a helpful website – get it out.

The first thing to consider at this point is just how much content the average pupil is expected to digest in a week. If you want to really dig into this, calculate roughly how many words are in front of you – in some weeks, it can be close to a short book. Now, sort that content into three piles.

The first pile is easy and should only be content that you have created yourself from scratch – easy. In an ideal world, this will be the largest pile because this will be the most personalised, accurately levelled and impactful content (or at least it will be by the end of this book).

In your second pile, place all the content that you downloaded or was created by a third party. This pile will form the beginning of your third pile, so it shouldn't take too long to sort this one out.

Your third pile is perhaps the most important. Go through your second pile and treat it like one of those self-help declutter-my-house type books. What content in your second pile could actually have been created by you instead if time wasn't an issue? Move this into the third pile.

At this juncture, I think I should make an important point. I was a teacher for nearly a decade and few things annoyed me more than somebody telling me to do something that would increase my workload, especially if they no longer worked in a classroom. I promise this isn't what I'm doing. Your third pile isn't going to become a pile of content that you absolutely must create yourself every single time. This is simply an exercise in reflecting on how much content your pupils access in an average week and whether you can use this to your advantage. By the end of this book, any content that you are creating should be quicker and more effective than before: this book will be a timesaver!

In front of you, you hold the evidence that answers the question with which we began this chapter. In your classroom, you are the most prolific and influential author. It doesn't all have to be about you; you can, and should, use content that others have created in your classroom. This is a vital element of your planning. However, you most definitely should be considering the impact that your own content can and, by the end of this book, will have.

CONNECTING TO YOUR CLASS

When I first started writing fiction, I did so because I wanted to challenge the children in my class to use more of the grammar and structural elements we were discussing in class. As I turned that initial short story into a longer novel, I began to read it to my class. It was a first draft and the first full-length story I'd ever written in earnest, and it told. The structure was loose, the characters underdeveloped and I hadn't found my author's voice at that point. None of that mattered.

The children in my class were excited to hear more every day simply because I, their teacher, had written it. This extends to everything you create for your class. How often do we, as teachers, celebrate the fact that we have written something? Most teachers understand the importance of demonstrating to our classes that we are readers – whether that takes the form of reading passionately to them in class or discussing books that we are reading at home. But how many of us do the same with our writing? Do you ever sit down and discuss how you came up with the idea for the model text you are about to place in front of them? Or how much you struggled to work out a way to include passive voice naturally?

If you are only or primarily taking content from third parties, where is the connection for your pupils? It's like only ever using audiobooks during story-time. Embrace the fact that you are a content creator, that you are, in a small way, an author, and I guarantee that you will notice a difference in engagement from that fact alone.

The impact from creating your own content isn't restricted to your English lessons. As a teacher, I lost count of the number of times I sat at my computer desperately searching for an information sheet on something really specific – let's say, the Taj Mahal – that was at just the right level for my class, that included all the information that I wanted them to extract and that was just the right length. I probably spent more time searching for that flawless content than it would have taken me to write one from scratch. Ultimately, I ended up settling for a text that wasn't quite perfect.

I wouldn't be surprised if one of your piles has content in it that has been created for a series of maths lessons. Consider a theoretical maths lesson, particularly one involving word problems. How often, when a child puts their hand up and says they can't answer a question, is it because they can't do the maths, or how often is because they don't understand what maths actually needs to take place because they can't comprehend the text?

If you took the time to carry out the Teacher Task above, you will know that you either create, or have the chance to create, content for a broad range of activities. It isn't just about writing a 500-word text for an English unit; it is so much more.

Throughout this book, I will refer to 'model texts'. For the purposes of what we are doing, I am referring to any teacher-created content at all, anything that ended up in one of your piles. I'll spend a lot of time looking at the impact on reading and particularly writing in English lessons, but the concepts are relevant to all subjects. When you read the chapters on engagement and impact, the impact of the content will be same whether the lesson is English or the life cycle of a river.

In the next chapter, we will look at why shifting the balance to more teacher-created content is so important.

2

IS TEACHER–CREATED CONTENT THAT IMPORTANT?

In Chapter 1, we looked at the opportunities you have as a teacher to create content for your class. With that in mind, it's worthwhile considering why it is worth your time to do this. There is a smorgasbord of content out there to download and utilise, not to mention shelves of fantastic books by people paid to write for children. So, why should you bother to create your own?

CUSTOMISED CONTENT

According to 2019 research by the National Literacy Trust (National Literacy Trust, 2019), in that year, 383,755 children in the UK did not have a book of their own at home. Disadvantaged children were more than 50 per cent less likely to own a book than their peers (9.3 per cent vs 6 per cent). If children aren't reading at home, then what they read in school becomes even more important. Most schools are great at providing access to rich, engaging texts, but these aren't written specifically for your class. They can't tap into children's interests or plug the gaps you have recognised (often after hours of data analysis or marking). Your texts can.

Chapter 6 will look in more detail at why books alone can't achieve this, but for now, trust me when I say that your content matters.

On some level, we know this as teachers. For example, a quick search for 'model texts' on the TES Resources page brings back over 9,000 teacher-generated resources, either free or paid for. Between them, they have thousands of downloads. As there is definitely an understanding that teacher-generated resources have value, why is it so much more difficult to value our own?

Suppose you are only downloading content from other creators. In that case, you will inevitably run into the same problems as only using published texts. The content might suffice for what you need, but it won't be tailored to your class and it won't have the level of impact that it potentially could.

One of the cornerstones of this book is the importance of analysing the reading level of the content you create, and exploring the impact and importance of this within your classroom. When you write your own content, you are in control of that. As research for this book, I analysed a selection of the resources available on TES, some paid and some free. Of the texts I looked at, only one had a reading level within the age group it was suggested for. Even that text wasn't entirely reading-level-appropriate – the text was recommended to be used with Years 5 or 6, but had a reading level of mid-Year 6. If you are concerned with the reading level of your content (Part 2 will show exactly why you should be), you can't rely on third-party content to help with this.

Again, I want to point out that there is nothing wrong with using content created by others. It saves time in a job that offers very little and, more often than not, they do a good enough job.

When it comes to maths, for instance, there is less nuance in the content you need. A sheet of twenty multiplication sums will be as effective whether you create it or if a random generator does. Even then, creating it yourself means that you can make sure there are plenty of 7s or 8s, or whichever table your group tends to need more practice with.

The point I'm hoping you take away is that, while this content will do a good enough job, your own content can go even further.

THE MAGIC RATIO

So, what is the magic ratio? How much should be created by yourself?

In an ideal but completely unrealistic world, all your content should be tailored to your class. However, by the time you've read this book and realised how quick and easy it can be to create personalised, effective content, you will be able to reach a point where you are writing at least half the content for your class.

TEACHER TASK 2

If you kept the three piles of content from Teacher Task 1, or if you took notes of how many pieces of work that were in each pile, you are ready to go with this quick task. If you didn't do Teacher Task 1, it might be worth going back to Chapter 1 and having a look to see what I'm talking about.

This task is simple enough. All I want you to do is look at the balance of content in your piles. If, like me, you are a fan of data, you have my permission to work out each pile as a percentage. If you're not, then go by eye.

In the week that you analysed, what was the ratio of content that you created to content that you found elsewhere? Were you anywhere near 50 per cent or was it skewed in one direction?

Now, combine the pile of stuff you created with the pile of content that you decided could have been created by you if you had the time. Imagine you now created that content, does that take you closer?

Getting to a point where you create most of your content won't happen overnight, but by recognising where you are with it is an important first step. You might have completed this task and realised you create far more content than you realised. Definitely give yourself a pat on the back and revel in the warm glow of your achievement. If you've realised that you perhaps want to create more, then rest assured you are not alone.

On its sign-up page, teacher resource website Twinkl offers over 600,000 resources ready and waiting for its subscribers (Twinkl Memberships, 2021). I've written over 600 reading comprehension texts, totalling over a quarter of a million words, for The Literacy Shed Plus. Teachers around the world rely on other content creators, and you should too. The important thing is to find the right balance.

When I was teaching, I often fell short of the half-and-half ideal. Finding your own balance is critical to this whole book. It's about saving you time and making what you create more effective, not about reaching some mythical ideal.

With all of this fresh in our minds, let's move on to Chapter 3 where we'll look at how your content links to the end of Key Stage expectations and the impact it can have on writing assessment and the SATs.

3

LINKING YOUR CONTENT WITH THE END OF KEY STAGE EXPECTATIONS

Throughout this book, I will be making references to the reading level of certain texts. Part 2 will go into much more detail about the different levelling systems that are available and how to use them effectively, but for now, you just need to know that they exist and that they provide an accurate level of reading difficulty that we can use to assess any text.

REAL-WORLD READING LEVELS

Before we move on to discuss the end of Key Stage SATs and the like, let's look at some real-world reasons why the reading level is important. First, reading outside of school isn't moderated and levelled with the same rigour as it is in school. In a 2000 study by Sheffield University (Clough, 2020), the average reading level of British newspaper articles ranged from Year 9 to almost Year 13.

With the rise of social media and the push to capture a reader's attention more quickly, it is conceivable that these reading levels will have dropped in recent years, but that isn't what I found with a quick piece of research.

The newspaper with the highest reading level in the Sheffield University study was *The Guardian* and the lowest was *The Sun*. I used the Flesch-Kincaid Scale to analyse the top ten articles on each newspaper's website, which gave a broad range of topics, including political, sporting and showbiz news. (While there may be more detailed reading level systems available now, the original study used the Flesch-Kincaid Scale, so I used the same. That way, the scores are directly comparable. Also, it remains one of the most popular and commonly used scales across the world, used by media outlets and governments to assess their content.)

More or less in line with the original report, articles published by *The Guardian* had an average reading level of almost Year 11, whereas articles on *The Sun* website had an average of mid-Year 8. The *BBC News* website, for comparison, had an average of around Year 9.

The children in your class are growing up in a world where opinion is often presented as fact, and being able to accurately read and comprehend popular news sources is more important than ever, so they need to be exposed to texts that build them up to that level.

Another interesting takeaway from this is that the average length of the articles was different as well. In *The Guardian*, the articles I analysed ranged from as little as 300 words all the way to nearly 2,500, with an average of around 970. In *The Sun*, they topped out at around 1,500 with an average of 600. Being able to read sustained articles is another reason why writing your own content for your classroom is important – you can measure and increase the length of your texts as needed to help improve this.

So, we know that being able to read at a certain level isn't just for the classroom, but it is definitely worth spending some time looking at just why it is so important within the classroom. For the rest of this chapter, that's what we are going to do.

CLASSROOM IMPACT

It's almost impossible to separate reading and writing within the classroom and the impact that one has on the other. Although a large part of this book is about the content you create for your classroom, I will be looking at the reverse – content created by your pupils (see Chapter 4 for a more in-depth look at this).

One of the main reasons that you will be creating content for your classroom will probably be to model the type of writing that you want to see being created by your pupils. By and large, that's the most common reason for creating model texts.

At the end of a writing unit, you might want your pupils to take what you have written and innovate it, rewrite it or whatever name you've given it. Ultimately, you want them to use yours as a scaffold to create their own. Reading level is critical here – if a pupil cannot comprehend what you have written, they are less likely to be able to accurately innovate from it. There is a real difference between decoding and comprehending, as I'm sure you are aware.

I once taught an EAL child in Year 6 who, despite their EAL status, could decode pretty much any Year 6 text I put in front of them. However, if I asked them a question about the text, even a relatively simple retrieval question, they were often unable to answer it. To anybody listening, they had 'read' the text perfectly, but they hadn't understood most of it.

This impact is the same with your texts and why analysing the reading level is so important. You may find that most of your class can decode your content, but are they able to comprehend it on a level that allows them to fully innovate it when the time comes?

When I first considered this and thought about my own class, I realised that most of my pupils were able to innovate to some degree, but then I remembered how many sessions we'd spent reading it as a class and breaking down each section. I remembered how hard I'd had to tease out some of the nuances I'd included. When I assessed the text I'd given them, it was too high by about a year. Even though they'd managed to come up with something by the end, I couldn't help but wonder how much further they'd have been able to take it had the text been at a level they could access more easily and quickly, particularly those pupils whose reading age was towards the lower end of the year. By giving them texts that only the greater depth readers could fully access, had I only succeeded in widening the gap?

Anybody who has taught Year 6 recently will be familiar with Morgan, Leigh and Frankie. For those who haven't, let me explain. The Standards and Testing Agency of the UK government provided a set of example texts in 2018 that Year 6 teachers can use to assess the writing of their pupils. The idea is to show what a lower-end piece of 'expected' Year 6 writing looks like (Morgan), a higher-end piece of 'expected' writing (Leigh) and a 'greater depth' piece of writing (Frankie) looks like. As somebody who went through the Year 6 writing moderation process, they were invaluable for making my own judgements and are the government's benchmark for what a Year 6 writer should look like.

Obviously, I decided to analyse them for their reading level. I looked at a sample of the texts for each example child, again using Flesch-Kincaid as the scale, and the results were very surprising.

For Morgan, who is an example of lower-end but still expected, the reading levels came out at around Year 5, which was to be expected. However, Leigh, who remember is still

Table 3.1   Flesch-Kincaid assessments for Key Stage 2 exemplar texts

Morgan (at expected)	Title	Flesch-Kincaid year group
Text 1	Dad	4
Text 2	Viking Day	6
Text 3	Letter	6
Text 4	Macbeth	5
Leigh (at expected)	**Title**	**Flesch-Kincaid year group**
Text 1	Short story	9
Text 2	Instructions	6
Text 3	Recount	10
Text 4	Information text	10
Text 5	Short story	7
Frankie (greater depth)	**Title**	**Flesch-Kincaid year group**
Text 1	Short story	4
Text 2	Description	7
Text 3	Explanation	8
Text 4	Newspaper report	8
Text 5	Diary	5
Text 6	Letter	11

writing at an expected standard, had an average reading level of Year 8–9. Some of the texts were at Year 10 reading level.

Frankie, writing at greater depth, perhaps ironically had an average of Year 7 (although one of the texts was at Year 11 level).

We will return to this point at the end of the chapter (and even more so in Chapter 4), but it is important to realise that a child writing at the expected level for Year 6 is going to be writing content that probably has a higher reading level than your own created content and the books they are reading.

With that in mind, let's dip our toes into the murky waters of SATs. Love them or loathe them, they are an important part of Year 2 and Year 6 and currently one of the ways in which you and your school are judged. It's therefore probably a good idea to have a look at the expectations within them.

SATS AND THEIR READING LEVELS

When I started assessing and analysing the SATs papers for this book, I focused mainly on the reading papers. It's a book about reading and reading levels, after all. Then I had a conversation with a fantastic lady at Renaissance® called Margaret Allen, who mentioned some research they had carried out on the maths papers as well.

For those who haven't heard of them, Renaissance is the company behind Accelerated Reader and the ATOS reading level assessment system (see Part 2). Margaret shares my enthusiasm for reading levels and their importance in the classroom, so she shared some of the data that they had collected – it was from that conversation that I began to analyse the maths papers as well.

In the end, I ended up assessing all of the reading papers back to 2016 (2017 for Key Stage 1) and using the Renaissance research for the maths papers for 2019 (Renaissance, 2021). I must admit, I expected the reading levels to be high enough to challenge the children, but the actual reading levels I found were surprising.

KEY STAGE 1

The reading level for the 'reading prompt' Reading Paper 1 texts for Key Stage 1 would be affected by the fact that the text is broken up by the questions, so the children are reading, and therefore comprehending, in much smaller blocks. Instead, I concentrated on the Reading Paper 2 texts, which are more sustained pieces of writing and require the children to read and comprehend for longer periods.

One of my first takeaways was the length of the texts (you'll notice that this is a recurring theme). Discounting poetry, the shortest text was back in 2017 and was 240 words. That year, children had to read around 720 words in total. It was much higher in 2018, even though it had a short poem, with a total of over 1,100 words. In 2019, children were required to read, give or take, 875 words. These totals are only for the reading texts. They don't take into account the reading required for the questions themselves. In 2019, the questions added over 400 extra words to be read by the children. This means that, of the total word count in 2019, a third were taken up by the questions.

Even though this book is primarily about considering reading levels, it's also about the importance of creating your own content because of the opportunities it gives you. I've mentioned it before, and I'll no doubt mention it many times again, that one of the key benefits to creating your own content is that you can start to build up the reading stamina of the pupils in your class. Whether 1,500 words is too many for a 6-year-old to read and respond to in 40 minutes is outside the scope of this book, but it is currently the reality that we need to prepare pupils for.

As with reading levels, being able to read for a sustained period is an important life skill, so this isn't something that is simply 'for the SATs', but knowing where the benchmark is can only make things easier for teachers and pupils alike.

So, what about the reading levels? If you haven't already cheated and looked at the table in Appendix D, you're perhaps in for a surprise. First, on any scale used to measure the reading level, it has remained consistent since 2017. Unfortunately, that consistent reading level is around Year 4. This means that the texts in the Key Stage 1 Reading Paper 2, sat by 6-year-old children, have a consistent reading level of Year 4. Let that sink in. Now, multiply that staggering information by the fact that the texts are perhaps longer than anything they've read before, it paints a pretty startling picture.

Here's the thing: every year, roughly 75 per cent of pupils in England pass the reading SATs (DfE, 2019), so it's clearly not too hard. However, look at your data, look at your work-load and how hard you are working with your pupils to get them to that point. SATs aren't everything, nor should they be, but they are a worry for many teachers, parents and pupils. The single reason that I am highlighting the data in this chapter is to point out where the bar is set. If your teacher-created content can help to bridge that gap a little more easily – whether that's with increased reading stamina or access to slightly higher-levelled texts – it can help to reduce your workload and the burden on your pupils, and will only make that process easier for all of you.

Just as an add-on to this, the questions for the 2019 Reading Paper 2 also came out with a reading level of Year 4.

KEY STAGE 2

Key Stage 1 SATs aren't the only ones with high word counts (I did warn you I'd keep bang-ing this drum). Since 2016, the total word count has slowly crept up by around 300 words; the 2019 reading paper totalled over 2,000 words without including the questions (they added nearly 950 additional words). All of this needs to be read and responded to within an hour.

If a child has a reading speed of 90 words per minute, that means they will be spending over half their time just reading and comprehending the text and questions. This doesn't even take into account any stamina or focus issues that they may face reading for so long. The first text in the 2019 test required pupils to read around 1,000 words, including questions.

A total of 90 words per minute is around the speed at which children can begin to com-prehend what they are reading and stop focusing on decoding (DfE, 2021); and children reading below that speed may qualify for additional time. At that speed, it would mean reading continuously for just over 11 minutes without a pause. They then have to do that two more times and answer around 39 questions on top of that.

Let's do some maths. At 90 words per minute, 3,000 words would take just over 33 minutes to read. Pupils have 60 minutes to complete the paper, leaving 27 minutes to answer 39 questions. That means they have roughly 42 seconds per question if they read and answer at a consistent pace without any pauses.

TEACHER TASK 3

This one is more of an observation task than you carrying out any work. All you are look-ing for is to see how long the pupils in your class can read for. Think of it as almost like a long-distance run for reading.

Set your class off reading their reading books (they need to have a text that will last long enough, so reading comprehension sheets won't work) and watch them closely. Which children can read for 11 minutes without glancing up from their book or staring into space? Which ones can get their head down and go the distance?

Now, do the same thing yourself. Choose a book and set yourself a timer for 11 minutes. Can you read for that amount of time without getting eye strain or need to look away at all? It's a lot harder than you might think.

So, your approach needs to be two-pronged. Increasing reading speed is important, but largely beyond the scope of this book. However, increasing reading stamina with longer texts, as I've already droned on about, is something that you will take control of once you begin to create more of your own content more efficiently. This will also have the added benefit of starting to increase fluency and reading speed, especially if it is tied in with focused support in these areas.

Next, we need to consider the reading levels. These are more in line with year-group expectations than the Key Stage 1 papers, but only just.

Just like the Key Stage 1 papers, the reading levels for Key Stage 2 reading papers have remained more or less consistent. Other than a high average of upper Year 8 in 2016, the Flesch-Kincaid levels have been between Year 6 and Year 7 ever since. However, there is a text in each year's paper that is much higher. The non-fiction texts in the 2017 and 2018 papers were at Year 8 level and the non-fiction text in the 2019 paper came out as Year 10. It is possible that these levels were pushed up by the technical vocabulary, but comparing them with scores from other systems, they were still higher than Year 6.

Perhaps more surprising is the data we get when we look at the maths SATs papers. The reading levels across the arithmetic and two reasoning papers for 2019 averages out at Year 6 level. Again, this is at the age expected level, but it does mean that if children aren't read-ing at that level, or haven't been exposed to texts at that level, then they are going to spend more time trying to comprehend the questions and less time showing what they can do from a maths perspective.

In Chapter 6, we will explore in more detail why this is an important thing to be aware of, but it highlights, along with the information we've looked at about newspapers, the need for children to be exposed to texts at the appropriate level. If the first time they see a text at Year 6 level is in the SATs or when they're reading a newspaper, then their comprehension and ability to access that text will be limited.

WHAT TO TAKE AWAY FROM THIS

The takeaway from all of this, then, is broad. There is certainly a discrepancy between the reading level of the texts that children are expected to write (if we use Morgan, Leigh and Frankie as an example) and what they are expected to read. There is also a trend towards increasingly higher word counts in SATs papers. While the Key Stage 2 SATs reading levels are broadly in line with the children's age, the Key Stage 1 papers are significantly higher.

Getting pupils to read at a Year 6 level isn't just the job of a Year 6 teacher. Ensuring that they are exposed to correctly levelled texts throughout Key Stage 1, Key Stage 2 will ensure that they are moving forward all the time. This is why it's so important that consideration is given to this aspect of your teacher-created content; being aware of it means that you can adjust and create accordingly.

In the next chapter, we will move on to looking at how your correctly levelled content can impact the effectiveness of peer- and self-assessment when it comes to writing.

4

THE IMPACT OF TEACHER-CREATED CONTENT ON PEER- AND SELF-ASSESSMENT

Asking children in your class to assess their own or each other's work is a critical part of improving their writing skills. However, it isn't without its problems as a process, but luckily the techniques and systems you will learn about in this book can have a positive impact on these areas as well.

REMOVING FRUSTRATION

We've all had those lessons where we've asked the pupils to swap work with their partners and peer-assess it. We might ask them to give it three stars and a wish or to fill in a more structured feedback grid, but ultimately there are always cases where the extent of the feedback is along the lines of:

Needs neater handwriting.

Check your spelling.

Or the eternally positive:

Really good.

It's frustrating for us as teachers and some of it is certainly down to a touch of laziness from some of the children. But, consider it another way, knowing what we know from Chapter 3. Let's imagine a Year 6 class sitting down to peer-assess each other's work. If the author of a piece of work is a child writing at the expected standard, then the evidence from Morgan and Leigh suggests that the reading level of their work is going to sit somewhere between Year 6 and Year 10.

Now, let's consider their partner who has to read, comprehend and then feed back on improvements for the piece of writing. If they are used to accessing texts at a Year 6 level, and they can read and comprehend at that level, then there is a chance that they will be able to access the text in front of them.

If, however, they aren't used to reading Year 6 texts (more in Chapter 6), or their reading level is below their age expectation, there is a high chance that they won't be able to fully access the text in front of them. If this is the case, is it any wonder that they can't provide detailed feedback or pick out structural or grammatical improvements? If they are struggling to fully understand what is written, how can they know whether it makes sense or whether it is in a consistent tense?

How often do we, as teachers, partner up children from different ends of the spectrum for this task as well? I've done it and I would guess that most of us have. Perhaps we placed the greater depth child with somebody working just below expected in a bid to 'inspire' them, to show them what Year 6 writing looks like. When we do that, are we actually rendering the whole process pointless because of the disparity between the reading level of the writing and the reading level of the reader? I'd argue yes.

WHAT ABOUT THEIR OWN WORK?

The same could be argued, ironically, for self-assessed work. Even though they have written the writing that they are trying to assess, if there is a difference between the reading levels of themselves and their writing, then that will have an impact on what they can access. This is especially true if they are returning to their work on a separate day.

One of the pieces of advice that all authors are given at some point in their career – normally early on – is to put a manuscript in a drawer (probably a metaphorical one now that everything is digital) once the first draft is complete. Leave it for a few weeks, we are all told, and then return to it with fresh eyes. Sure enough, you spot significantly more errors and areas for improvement than if you did it straight away because you naturally forget what you have written. I've read my own books a year or so after publication, and I can't remember writing half of it, even though I clearly did.

Children work the same. If they wrote something a few days before, then returning to it will be almost like reading somebody else's writing. Therefore, the difference between reading levels will be more apparent.

I've focused here on Year 6 simply because we have firm, government-approved evidence of the reading level of Year 6 writing. The same impact will be felt throughout the school, though. It's important that you don't take away that this is simply something to consider in Year 6.

BEYOND WRITING

It's also something to consider outside of writing lessons. Maybe you've asked your class to use the internet to research the Inca civilisation and are growing frustrated that all they are doing is copying and pasting into a document. Perhaps both you and your class are growing frustrated that, even though they are searching for the correct term, they aren't finding the answers you want them to. How much of this is down to a lack of ICT knowledge and how much is down to lazy searching, but also how much is down to the fact that the content is just too hard for them to comprehend and filter out the important facts? If all they are reading is a block of words that they can't understand at a deeper level, how can they reword it into their own content?

This may all seem like a lot of doom and gloom, but it needn't be. We can't impact the reading level of their writing – this is set by the end of year expectations – but we can make sure that they are regularly being exposed to texts that are at the same level and that prepare them for this.

Another step to take is to have a rough idea of the reading level of the texts that your children are writing. Once you know this, you can decide whether it is more beneficial to pair children for peer-assessment activities based on a match in reading and writing levels.

As with everything in this book, the idea is to give yourself useful information, not to add more onerous data-collection activities on to your already packed plate. This isn't something you need to do all the time and there's no need to commit to always pairing the same children for peer-assessment. I still believe that it is good practice to show children at both ends of the attainment spectrum what the other children are writing, but it's something to bear in mind when you are planning these sessions.

TEACHER TASK 4

If you haven't read Part 2 yet, then stick a bookmark or scrap of paper here and return to it once you've read up on how to level pieces of writing.

For this task, we are going to have a look at the reading levels of some of the writing in your class. It's important to remember that this isn't an assessment of the writing itself. If the reading level is lower than you expect, it shouldn't impact your judgement of that child or their writing; there are many reasons why a reading level can be lower than expected.

One of the easiest and most time-efficient ways to assess the text is to have it in a digital format already; if your class have typed their work, then this is perfect (although, do look out for typos and other errors that might have crept in when typing it up). If not, then it shouldn't take too long to type it up yourself. Remember, you only need a few texts. I wouldn't recommend assessing an entire class unless you really wanted to see the data.

Once you've worked out the reading levels, have a look at how they compare to the texts that the children are reading at other points in class. Use one of the book-finder systems (Chapter 6) to see if they line up with any books that the children might be reading.

This is where your texts are important. There will inevitably be reading-level gaps between the texts that your class are reading and the texts they are writing. Once you are familiar with the reading level of your own texts, you can start to bridge that gap.

Obviously, this won't fix all the problems you might encounter with peer- and self-assessment. One child once said to me during a self-assessment session: 'If I knew how to make it better, I'd have done that the first time.' While they may have had a point, recognising areas for improvement, both in your own work and that of a peer, isn't easy. It's one of the reasons that editors get paid the big bucks. However, if you are asking children to consider those difficult concepts *while also not being able to comprehend the text that they are supposed to improve*, the situation is all the more difficult.

I've said it a few paragraphs ago, but I think it needs repeating: the idea here isn't to check the reading level of every piece of work that your children write, nor to fret unduly about your peer-assessment pairings. As the saying goes: 'Knowledge is power.' If you occasionally check in with the reading level of some of your children's writing, then you might choose to alter some of the pairings or scaffold sessions differently.

It isn't just peer- and self-assessment that can be impacted by your teacher-created content. In the next chapter, we will have a quick look at the impact that they can have on engagement and behaviour as well.

5

THE IMPACT ON BEHAVIOUR AND ENGAGEMENT

Classroom behaviour is a delicate balance nurtured throughout the year with your class. So what impact, if any, can your teacher-created content have on such a nuanced area?

First, this isn't a new behaviour management strategy that promises to revolutionise the relationships you have with your class or the behaviour that you experience within it, even if such a silver bullet actually exists. Instead, it's just a way of considering the impact that your words can have.

To me, most of this seems fairly obvious, so this won't be a long chapter, but I wanted to highlight it because sometimes it's easy to forget the consequences and benefits of some of the smaller things that we do as teachers.

RESILIENCE TAKES TIME

Resilience and perseverance are key life skills that teachers spend a lot of their time trying to instil into their pupils, but most primary children haven't mastered them by the time they leave (nor have many adults, to be fair). So, if something is exceptionally difficult, then what do we all naturally want to do? We want to give up and retreat to something that we know we can do. We disengage from the task.

What happens, then, if you ask a Year 2 class to read a text that is too difficult? Many of those who will inevitably struggle will disengage, and once they have done that, you will have to fight to get them back on board with the task. Invariably, your sanity and their behaviour will suffer.

The flip side of the coin is equally destructive. If something is too easy, we equally navigate away from it more quickly than if there is a challenge there. How often do we play a computer game that we can beat in seconds? James Paul Gee noted in a series of essays on using video games for learning that children in particular thrive on the challenge that a game provides them. If it is too easy, they will switch off and move on. If the challenge is too great, then the result will be the same. That's why computer games work so well as teaching aids (Gee, 2005).

(If you haven't read any of James Gee's work, finish this book first, then seek it out. His ideas on using computer games in class are really worth considering.)

We know through our own experience as teachers that this holds true in the classroom, along with the fact that disengaged children often behave in a way that entertains them and their peers at the expense of usual behavioural expectations. In other words, they act out.

GOLDILOCKS

In the 1930s, the Russian psychologist Lev Vygotsky put forward the notion of a Zone of Proximal Development or ZPD. This has been refined over the years and is now believed by many to be the zone in which children learn and engage most effectively with their learning (Fletcher, 2018). In simple terms, children learn best when there is a challenge that can be met. If it's too hard, they enter the 'panic zone' and can't engage. Too easy, and there is no motivation. Think of it as a Goldilocks zone, where it's not too hot and not too cold.

For the most part, the content that you put in front of your class needs to try to sit in that ZPD. Over a whole class, that will be a relatively broad zone, but this is no different from any other subject or part of your teaching. When you put together a presentation for your class, you ensure that the information is accessible, engaging and yet still poses a challenge. When producing a sheet of questions for maths, you will ensure that there is sufficient scaffolding in place to put the questions in each child's ZPD.

Knowing about the reading level of your teacher-created content is just another way of doing the same thing. Don't forget, this book isn't just about the content that you create for English lessons; it is pertinent to any and all content that you create for your pupils to access. Remember when we talked about those theoretical maths problems in Chapter 1? Are your children disengaging from their maths work because the questions are too difficult to read? The same goes for research content for history, geography, RE or wherever else you are using it.

When it comes to your own class, their ZPD will be different from the class next door or in the next school. That's why it's important to understand what the reading levels you get mean (see Chapter 7 for a full breakdown of this) and how it applies to your class. It might mean that you scaffold the text differently for some children or reduce or increase the reading level for others.

However you choose to use the information you glean from calculating the reading level of your own content, the fact that you are aware of it in the first place is a big step towards, increasing the engagement of your class with those texts.

But, and perhaps this is the biggest but in the book, engagement isn't only going to come from an appropriate reading level. Ask yourself another question for me, if you don't mind. Would you rather read a book about an anonymous spy who travels the world and defeats a super villain, or one where your parent, or best friend, or colleague does the same? It's not as difficult or time-consuming as it sounds to create the latter across your school. The end result will be more engagement from your class (we'll go into lots of detail about this in Chapter 18).

A REAL CONNECTION

When you use third-party content, you are giving the children in your class a standard text that has no connection to them. When you create your own, with a little bit of imagination and some forward planning (see Chapter 18), you can include things that nobody else in the world can in order to connect with your class. It could be you on the adventure or one of them. Perhaps a reward for persevering with their writing might be a chance to appear in next week's model text, or maybe the head teacher is on the rampage in Victorian London.

For very little extra effort, you can create content that contains characters, situations and ideas that appeal specifically to your class. If you are having particular trouble with one child's behaviour in English, but you know that they love trains, write a text that focuses heavily on that. Chapter 14 drills down on what I think is an important consideration when it comes to linking content to a topic that can have a real impact on improving engagement in these ways.

Hopefully, you can see that the link between teacher-created content and behaviour and engagement is less spurious than it seems at first. It won't fix every problem, and there's nothing incredibly new here, but it seems to me just one more reason why you are the most influential author in your classroom.

In the final chapter in Part 1, we will move on to look at what impact published books can have on reading levels and why they might not be the answer to all the issues we've raised.

6

WHAT IMPACT CAN PUBLISHED BOOKS HAVE?

I want you to think about the reading books that you have offered to your class over the past few years. Why did you choose them? You might have picked them because they tied in nicely with your topic or because they are the books that have always been read in that year group within your school. You might have chosen them because you felt they were appropriate for that year group. But at any point, did you consider the reading level of these texts?

There's a big difference between reading age and the age that the content is appropriate for. We'll discuss this more in Part 2, but it's important that you begin this chapter with the knowledge that appropriate content doesn't always mean appropriate reading age.

TEACHER TASK 5

Many teachers pick books for their class based on reading spines that are either embedded within their school or that they've been recommended. This is a great way to discover books that you might not have considered and can help to find books that tie in with history and geography topics. It's also the reason why I've chosen the following books. They appear in lots of recommended lists and in lots of classrooms.

I also want to preface this task, and really this chapter, with the caveat that I think reading high-quality books such as these in class is vital, whether it's the teacher reading to the class or the children reading themselves. They are essential and all the books on this list are, in my humble opinion, amazing. So please don't let this activity and the conclusions we'll draw lead you to think that I think anything differently.

The books below are all popular across the school. What I would like you to do is think carefully about each book and consider where you would use it in school to 'teach' from. I've added quotation marks around 'teach' because I really mean 'where it would appear in the classroom'.

It might be that the text is used to inform guided reading or it might just be as a reading-for-pleasure text at a set time in the day. It might also not be read as a whole class at all, but rather introduced on the class bookshelf.

Generally, though, it will be where you would decide to use it with your class. I also want you to think about *why* you chose it. Was it because it ties in with something else you know is taught in that year? Was it because of the content or the text difficulty?

Have a think about these books:

Wonder (2012) (R.J. Palacio)

Charlotte's Web (1952) (E.B. White)

Of Mice and Men (1937) (John Steinbeck)

Street Child (1993) (Berlie Doherty)

Varjak Paw (2003) (S.F. Said)

Cogheart (2016) (Peter Bunzl)

The Hunger Games (2008–2010; 2020) (Suzanne Collins)

Once you've sorted them all out, let's move on.

This is always a great task to carry out with the staff in a school because there will always be a difference of opinion and the discussion that surrounds it is both fascinating, but also critical to understanding the broader points of this chapter.

You might have been hampered in this task if you didn't have a copy of the texts in front of you. If you do decide to do it at a staff meeting, try to get copies of the texts so that staff who aren't familiar with the books can have a skim through.

One thing that does tend to happen is that teachers focus on two things when carrying out this task, and you'll hear a lot of conversations along the lines of: 'It's about the Romans, so that would go into Year 3 where they teach Ancient Rome.' Or: 'It's a bit scary/deals with complex issues, so definitely Year 6.'

These are valid arguments and the point of this chapter isn't to discourage or diminish those points. Of course, a text that supports a topic will naturally be placed with it; it makes a lot of sense and is a great idea.

But, and it's a big but, there is another level to consider. The reading age of the books is as follows (remember, this is the structural reading-level age, not the content-appropriate age):

- *Wonder* – Year 4
- *Charlotte's Web* – Year 4
- *Of Mice and Men* – Year 4

- *Street Child* – Year 4 (it's harder to read than *Wonder*)
- *Varjak Paw* – Year 3
- *Cogheart* – Year 4
- *The Hunger Games* – Year 4

A NOTE ON READING LEVELS

There are several different systems for getting the reading level of a text and we'll discuss them all in more detail in Part 2 of the book. However, two of the biggest companies (Lexile® and Renaissance®) also have systems that provide reading levels for pretty much all children's books. Currently, both are free services that don't require registration and are well worth looking into.

Renaissance's system is called the Accelerated Reader Bookfinder and provides a number rating called an ATOS Book Level that links roughly with the American grade system. The higher the number, the harder the text. You can use the system at www.arbookfind.com.

Lexile's system is called Find a Book and gives each book a Lexile rating between roughly 150 and 1600. The higher the level, the harder a book is to read. You can use this system by going to https://hub.lexile.com and clicking on Find a Book.

The reading levels given above were calculated using the Lexile system for consistency, but the results from the Renaissance system were the same.

Did you notice a pattern with the results? Were any of them close to where you thought you would teach them? It doesn't matter if not; that was the whole point of this task.

When we look in a little more detail at how the publishing industry works, these results shouldn't be too surprising. Books tend to be written and published for a broad age group rather than a specific age. For most Key Stage 2 readers, this is called mid-grade. This is generally considered to be readers aged 8–12 or Year 4 to Year 8. The reasons for this are financial – simply put, there are more readers to reach in the broader age bracket than if it was only written for Year 6 children.

ACCESSIBLE TO ALL

Mid-grade, then, is a broad range of readers. The structural decoding ability of a Year 4 is vastly different from a Year 8, especially when you take into consideration things like inference.

To make sure that a mid-grade book is accessible to the entire range, it has to be written with a reading level that a child on the bottom rung can access. Ergo, a significant proportion of mid-grade books, and therefore books that you are likely to have in your classroom, will have a reading age of Year 4.

You can check it out for yourself using the systems above and some of the books in your class.

THE IMPACT ON YOUR CLASS

I can hear you asking the obvious question: 'If I think all these books are great and that I agree you should definitely be using them in your class, why am I raising the issue?'

Over the book so far, we have already recognised how important it is to expose the children in your class to texts at an appropriate level. It is sometimes easy to fall into the trap of thinking that a complex narrative that uses brilliant vocabulary and is awash with implied information means that it is also difficult to decode on a structural level. A great example of this is *Wonder*. However, as we have just seen, the reading level is only Year 4.

Consider the following two paragraphs that I have written:

Paragraph 1: *The boy, who, despite his mother's repeated instructions, had still refused to wear his coat, was finding that walking to school (an already unwelcome task) was even less pleasant when soaked through to the skin by the dreary afternoon rain that hadn't let up since the previous Monday.*

Paragraph 2: *It wasn't the first time that the strange girl had defended her. She always seemed to be there when Claire needed her to be. There was something about her that encouraged friendship. There was a first time for everything.*

Paragraph 1 consists of a single sentence that basically tells the reader that a boy is getting wet and miserable on the way to school because he refused to wear his coat. There's not a huge amount of information to be inferred from it and the language is acceptable, but nothing spectacular.

Paragraph 2 contains four simple sentences. However, there is a lot to be inferred from it. Claire seems to struggle to make friends. Who is the mystery girl? Why is she always there? What about her encourages friendship? And so on.

It's clear that content-wise, at least, the second paragraph is probably going to be more appropriate for an older age group. However, the first paragraph has a reading level of around Year 7 compared to around Year 4 for the second paragraph.

Bearing all that in mind, consider your class again for me. If the main content that they are reading consists of texts that you have downloaded, content that you have created but that might not be at the correct reading level, or books that we now know probably aren't at the appropriate reading level, then what is going to fill that gap and give them exposure to texts that *are* at the correct reading level?

If you work in a school that uses Accelerated Reader (also by Renaissance), then you will be familiar with this concept already. Their system is based on matching children's individual reading levels with published books at a similar level. It works well and solves some of this problem, although your content is still likely to be far more personalised and impactful and should still be considered.

If you don't work in a school that uses Accelerated Reader or any other system, then it's perhaps even more important that you consider using the tools I mentioned to get an idea of the reading levels on your class bookshelf.

WHAT IF I'M AN ENGLISH LEAD?

A good question! If you're an English lead or coordinator in your school and hadn't considered this before, then I would definitely recommend having a look into it. It can be a huge job analysing all the books on all the classroom bookshelves, so why not start with the books that are taught in each year group?

Think back to the imaginary conversation we had earlier, where the book about the Romans was put into Year 3 because that's where they teach it. If that book has a reading level that is higher than Year 3, are they really benefiting from having it there if they can't access it? You may decide that they are, and that is a perfectly valid response, but at least you'll know. If every book that is taught in Year 3 is too high, then you can start to tweak the reading spine for that year group to bring it more in line with the children's own reading levels, if needed.

When you begin to consider this and to look at it across the school, you might find that it inspires you to refresh the books that you use. With the Romans, you might consider looking for a new set of books that cover the topic at a lower reading level, or you might set out to find a set of books that cover the slave trade for Year 6 that are at a higher reading level than the ones you've got.

It might only be that you look into it when you come to buy new books, but having that information at your fingertips can make sure that there is a range of reading levels available across the school.

READING ALOUD

There is an addendum to all of this, of course, and that concerns who is doing the reading. The assumption for this chapter is that the texts in question will be being read by the children themselves. After all, it's their reading level that matters when accessing a text.

This gives you a great opportunity. If the teacher is reading a text to the class, either as a reading-for-pleasure activity or as part of a literacy unit, then the reading level of the text is less important because the teacher will access the text, and their voice and expression will help to translate it to the pupils. This means that you can read up or down in level and still make it work.

If the reading level is too high, then the teacher has the chance to break down more complex sentences and structures and even use them as a teaching point (although I would discourage this during reading-for-pleasure, which should just be about enjoying the story). If the level is too low, then the teacher can pick out the implied information where appropriate.

I started this chapter with a caveat that I think high-quality texts like these are vital to classrooms, and I stick by that. They teach story structure, rich vocabulary, creative thinking, beautiful personification and other imagery, important life lessons, the need for pacing and author voice, and so much more. Not everything is about reading levels, so long as we understand that books might not be filling in the gaps that we thought they were.

With that, we have stumbled to the end of Part 1 of the book, and I don't know about you, but I need a biscuit.

Through this first part you've learned about the following:

- Where and why you have opportunities to create content for your class.
- Why teacher-created content is so important to your class.
- How it all links to end of Key Stage expectations.
- How creating your own content can help with assessment, behaviour and engagement.
- What impact published books can have on your class's reading level.

That's a lot to get through, but you should be able to see by now why it's so critical.

In Part 2, we will look at the systems that exist for levelling texts in more detail, along with how they work and how you can use this information to adjust your own content. It promises to be a blinder, so I'll see you there!

PART 2

LEVEL IT: WHAT DOES LEVELLING YOUR CONTENT LOOK LIKE?

7

WHAT IS A READING LEVEL ASSESSMENT?

THE BEGINNINGS

In the 1940s, Rudolf Flesch developed a formula for calculating the 'readability' of a text. Over time, the formula was developed to become the Flesch-Kincaid reading ease and Flesch-Kincaid grade level systems. The reading ease formula gives a text a score out of 100, with 100 being incredibly easy to read and 1 impossible. The grade level gives a text an American school grade level.

Throughout this chapter, we'll be dealing with systems that tend to give results linked to the American school grade system. I'll make it clear when I'm discussing grade level (US school grade) and year level (UK year group level), but the conversion is easy enough to do: the UK year groups are 1 less than the US grade. So, Grade 4 is Year 3, Grade 8 is Year 7, and so on.

According to the people at readable.com, the system is widely used around the world by everyone, from advertising companies to the US Navy (readable.com, 2021). The premise behind the system is simple: it's free to use and easily accessible. So why am I going to recommend two other systems instead?

THE MATHS BEHIND READING

The simplicity of Flesch-Kincaid is its downfall for what we are doing. The system is so simple that we can include the formula here for calculating the grade level.

$$0.39 \times (\text{total words/total sentences}) + 11.8 \times (\text{total syllables/total words}) - 15.59$$

You can see from the formula that the only things that Flesch-Kincaid is concerned with are total words, total sentences and total syllables. On the surface, this makes sense and is probably fine for many public-facing documents, which is where it tends to be used most.

The word 'monotonous' takes more brainpower (because it has more syllables) than 'boring'. However, no consideration is actually given to the words themselves.

Let's take this snippet of a much longer sentence from Charles Dickens's *Nicholas Nickleby*:

> *Mr Godfrey Nickleby purchased a small farm near Dawlish in Devonshire, whither he retired with his wife and two children . . .*

It generates a Flesch-Kincaid grade level of 11.1 and a reading ease of 51.2. Never mind the fact that a modern child might struggle with the word 'whither', the sentence structure itself is quite complicated. We'll discuss that more later on in this chapter.

Now, look at the following sentence:

> *He dizzily twizzles a judo jelly chequebook, near to showbiz kickboxers, jogging in Halifax with his dogs and two giraffes.*

The reading ease is pretty much identical. The grade level is marginally higher because there are slightly more syllables in the second sentence, but every word in there would be understandable by most Key Stage 2 children, yet the reading level is still within Year 10.

For fun, consider:

> *Kg ghyeojg heyaoghn k koeh naheo lwpahdntj, rpka ne lgpahnv abqxcpzngh, hfnadqm mp hnurngl fghu unf iane qwe mbx lgnadfg.*

It's utter nonsense typed out by me randomly to hit the same average word length. However, the system can't work out the syllables, so it gets a lower grade level of 7.6 (middle Year 6). It also has a reading ease score of 76.6, so if you can't read it, then I guess that is on you!

After all that, I think it's clear that we might need an alternative to the traditional method if we are going to make it relevant to our classroom.

THE COMPETITION

Through my own writing, I've discovered two systems that I believe work perfectly for what we are discussing in this book. They are the Lexile® system and the Renaissance® ATOS system. It's no coincidence that both of these also offer the book levelling systems that I recommended in Chapter 6 – they do what they do very well. There are differences between them that I'll cover later, but for now, I'll be focusing on these two.

When it comes to assessing the content we create for our classrooms, in an ideal world, we would want a system to consider several things when it assesses reading level:

* Sentence length.
* Sentence structure.
* Word choice.

- Content appropriateness.
- Interest level.

Unfortunately, we are never going to have a system that does all of those things. We know that sentence length and sentence structure can be quantified to a large degree. However, it's still hard to quantify in an algorithm all of the different permutations that a sentence might take and how difficult they would be – for instance:

It was a rainy day in Spain.

is an easier sentence to read than:

In Spain, it was a rainy day.

if only because the information isn't presented in sequential order. But is the second sentence more difficult than:

It was a rainy day; the clouds were grey.

Both the ATOS and Lexile systems are proprietary, so the exact methods behind their systems are closely guarded secrets; however, in my experience, they do both take into consideration the structure of the sentence *to some degree*. While greater weighting is given to sentence length and word complexity, sentence complexity definitely plays a part and will need to be considered. I'll discuss this more in Chapter 10.

Content appropriateness is another area where it is impossible for a system to define a level. Even on a macro level, it would be difficult to pinpoint exactly how to place content on the Holocaust, for instance. When you get to more nuanced issues around inferred meaning, slang and innuendo, etc., then it becomes even more impossible. The same can be said for interest level.

This is another tick in the box for why it's so important that you are creating content for your class where appropriate. You get to decide the content; you get to decide the interest level. You don't need a system to tell you if a text is content- or interest-appropriate if you've written it yourself.

The area where both systems really excel is with their consideration for word choice. Both use their own vast database of vocabulary, which assigns almost every word a commonality score. The more common a word is, the more likely a child is likely to have read it before, so the easier they should find it to read again. This means that words like 'showbiz' will have a lower score than a word like 'whither', as it should.

Vocabulary is also difficult to uniformly quantify, but the regularity with which children are exposed to a word is a very good metric. Context and life experience are also critical and harder to evaluate with an algorithm.

These *qualitative* measures are only really measurable by a human, but they greatly aid a child's reading. Throughout this book, whenever we've talked about a 'reading level', what we've really meant is perhaps better defined as a 'comprehension level'. According to the

DfE Statutory Guidance (DfE, 2014), pupils leaving Year 2 at the expected level should be able to decode most words fluently. Therefore, we need to separate the act of decoding from the more nuanced act of understanding.

A few years ago, I taught a child who had recently moved to England. They had a basic knowledge of the English language, but they definitely fell under the EAL umbrella. When I gave them a text levelled at Year 6 using the systems discussed here, they read every single word fluently. However, when I asked them a question about the text, they struggled. They had decoded fine, but their comprehension wasn't there because the combination of trying to translate and understand the vocabulary at the same time as comprehending more complicated sentence structures and language was too much.

When I gave the same child a text levelled at Year 4, they could answer most of the questions I asked because the cognitive load was lighter.

This is an important distinction because it highlights why vocabulary choice is a critical consideration for calculating an accurate reading level and why relying on sentence length, word length and syllables aren't enough when it comes to the context of children reading.

When that same child took a reading test that considered vocabulary, they emerged with a reading age of Year 4, which makes sense. It should also be pointed out at this point how language-specific all of this is. Their reading age in their native language was several years higher than their chronological age; the issue wasn't a broader comprehension issue but a language comprehension issue.

CONTEXT

Let's think about how this might look in real life. You have two children in your class, both of whom have taken a reading level test and come out at the same level. You put a text about dinosaurs in front of both of them. One of them answers most of the questions correctly, the other doesn't. What's the difference? The key might be their contextual knowledge. When you are assessing content for a reading level, it won't assess the contextual knowledge.

If child A has been fascinated by dinosaurs since they were a toddler, they might well have been reading, or have had read to them, books about dinosaurs. They will be familiar with words like 'palaeontologist', 'Jurassic', 'Cretaceous', 'aeon', 'period', 'evolution', and so on. When they read your dinosaur text, that language was completely in context for them, so they understood it.

Child B may never have come across those words before, so the text, while it was within their reading ZPD, caused them to struggle.

Consider the following paragraph from a report on the importance of reading level assessment (NGA/CCSSO, 2013):

Simultaneously with the work on quantitative metrics, additional fieldwork was performed with the goal of helping educators better judge the qualitative features of text complexity. In the CCSS, qualitative measures serve as a necessary complement to quantitative measures, which cannot capture all of the elements that make a text easy or challenging to read and are not equally successful in rating the complexity of all categories of text.

I would imagine that you are able to decode every word in that paragraph fluently, yet it probably made very little sense because it is entirely out of context. Had you read the rest of the report or had greater knowledge of the systems being discussed, your comprehension would have been greater.

The knowledge demands of a text are subjective, therefore, and vary from child to child, so they can't be assessed by a reading level algorithm. Not to labour a point I've made many times before, but one of the benefits of creating your own content is that you can ensure that all the content is contextually relevant for your class. Whatever trend or fad or interest in your group, or even down to the individual if you are creating intervention content, can be catered to. If the knowledge demand of the text is low, then overall comprehension will increase. I'll go into more detail about this in Chapter 13.

So, now we know what we *need* our system to do and what we can't expect it to do, what is out there to do just that?

LEXILE

The Lexile system gives you a result in numerical form between roughly 150 and 1600, followed by an L. For example, my book *The Halloween Parade* has a Lexile score of 850L. To access the Lexile Analyzer, you need to head to the Lexile Hub at https://hub.lexile.com.

Unfortunately, the Lexile Analyzer is no longer free. At the time of writing, it is currently $17.99 per year plus any taxes. Alongside this, the system only returns a result within a range, which is less useful. Due to these two restrictions, the Renaissance/ATOS system is the one I would recommend the most. However, you may prefer Lexile, so I've included information about it below.

PREMIUM SUBSCRIPTION

Currently $17.99 a year, this probably won't break the bank, but only you can decide whether it will offer you enough benefit to make it worthwhile. It allows you to analyse texts with a word count up to 500 words and gives you a breakdown of key vocabulary that is impacting the reading level, along with the text structures that are doing the same. This is a useful feature and something that none of the Renaissance/ATOS systems offer. However, if you read Chapter 10 of this book, you will get a breakdown of things to look out for and will soon become an expert at spotting them for yourself.

ANALYSING THE RESULTS

My biggest bugbear with the Lexile system is that the results you get are in a range. Through the Lexile Hub, you can access the Lexile Grade Level Charts, which give bands for each American school grade; however, these don't tie in with the banding you will get as a result. For instance, in Figure 7.1, you can see that the text I analysed came back with a result of

---

LEXILE RANGE 🔘
610L – 800L

The Lexile range generated is not a certified Lexile range and should only be considered an estimated Lexile range.

Figure 7.1   Lexile range 610L–800L

610L–800L, but the closest banding is either Grade 2 at 425L–795L or Grade 3 at 645L–985L, neither of which tell me where within that grade my text actually sits, which is important. The best you can get is a rough feel of where your content sits.

RENAISSANCE/ATOS

Renaissance are the people behind the Accelerated Reader programme, so they have a lot of knowledge about reading within schools. Their system is free, can be used without registering and gives accurate levels based on a range of criteria.

Sentence length and word complexity are the two heaviest weightings for Renaissance, but their algorithms also take into account the structure and reading order of a sentence. So, our example of a rainy day in Spain would show different levels for each of the three examples I gave.

The Renaissance system for assessing text level is called ATOS (as opposed to their Accelerated Reader system), and there are three different ways to check your text. Each one has a specific use case in mind, so it's important to understand the differences and to choose the correct one. All three can be accessed via www.renaissance.com/products/accelerated-reader/atos-and-text-complexity/.

For all of the ATOS systems, the level you are interested in is called the ATOS Book Level in the results. You might also need to look at the Average Word Length and Average Sentence Length if you need to adjust the level (see Chapter 10).

Results:	
File submitted:	a sample text.docx
ATOS Book Level:	3.9
AR Points	0.5
Word Count:	419
Average Word Length:	4.2
Average Sentence Length:	16.8
Language Selected:	English
Confirmation #:	2047487

Figure 7.2   ATOS Book Level results

ATOS FOR TEXT

This system allows you to either copy and paste your text into it or to upload a text file. With all the ATOS systems, your text file can be Microsoft Word format or Rich Text. The ATOS for the text system assumes that your text is part of a larger text, so it doesn't take into account the overall length of your text. This means that it is best used for snippets that you are going to use, perhaps from a book or part of a larger text you have created.

If you use this for a text that is complete – perhaps your entire 500-word model text – then you will find that you get higher levels than you expect. This is because a text that is quite complex but only 500 words will be easier for a child to read than a 20,000-word text that is that complex throughout. Because the content is assumed to be part of a larger text, it raises the level.

ATOS FOR BOOKS

Don't be confused by the title; this system is for short texts as well. The primary difference is that this one *does* take into account the overall text length and treats it as one complete text. I write a lot of comprehension texts for The Literacy Shed website and this is the system I always use. It's also the system I would recommend you to use for the content that you create. Because it treats it as a complete text, your reading level result will be much more accurate.

Unless you are copying a snippet from a book or longer text, I'd recommend you use this system.

ESTIMATED WORD COUNT

This system is basically a combination of the other two. If you are copying from another, longer text and know the total word count of the complete piece, you could use this system.

ANALYSING THE RESULTS

When you analyse a text with any of the ATOS systems, you are presented with a table at the bottom of the page (see Table 7.1) that breaks down the results by American grade and the access percentile. This is important and something to consider when you are analysing your own content.

The percentile columns tell you what percentile of your class will be able to access your text at that particular level. These are presented in the opposite way to what makes sense in my head, so I'll explain in case you are the same as I am.

The first column gives you the ATOS Book Level at which the bottom 25th percentile in your class will be able to access it. In this case, 'access' means comprehend roughly 70 per cent of the text. What this actually means is that, on average, 75 per cent of your class

Table 7.1   ATOS system percentile breakdown

| Grade | Instructional reading | | |
| | Bottom | Middle | Top |
	(25th percentile)	(50th percentile)	(75th percentile)
1	1.57	2.52	3.3
2	2.75	3.62	4.21
3	3.89	4.69	5.14
4	4.97	5.74	6.08
5	6.01	6.75	7.03
6	7.00	7.74	8.00
7	7.93	8.7	8.98
8	8.82	9.64	9.98
9	9.67	10.55	10.99
10	10.46	11.42	12.01
11	11.2	12.28	13.05
12	11.9	13.1	14.1

will be able to access it at that level (the bottom 25 per cent might struggle). The actual maths is slightly different, but for our intents and purposes, it's a good way to think of it.

At the other end, the third column tells you the ATOS Book Level, at which only those in the top 75th percentile (so the top 25 per cent of your class) will be able to access it. This is critical. It's possible to analyse a text and see that it fits within the Year 2 boundaries, but if it sits in the 75th percentile range, then the majority of your class will still struggle to access it at any meaningful level. It's also a very useful metric to consider if you are creating content for intervention groups or if your class as a whole has a lower or higher than average reading ability.

If you are writing content for a higher ability group, then you might want to ensure that the content has an ATOS Book Level within that 75th percentile banding, but if it's for a catch-up group, then it might be worth aiming for the 25th or 50th percentile range.

TEACHER TASK 6

You now know how to analyse your content and evaluate the results. Let's use that to analyse a piece of content that you've written for your class recently. Find a text that is at least 300 words and use one of the systems above to analyse it. If you've handwritten it, first, I applaud your dedication; my handwriting is illegible, but you will obviously need to type it up first.

When you've got your result back, have a look at where it fits on either the Lexile or Renaissance grade analysis sheets. The first check is whether it fits within your year group. If it's too low, that's not necessarily a bad thing (see Chapter 8), but if it's too high, then it's a good opportunity to look at why (see Chapter 11).

If it fits within your year group, and you used the Renaissance systems, have a look at where it fits. Which percentile of your class would be able to access it? Are you happy with where it fits?

If you fancy it, this is a great point to have a look at a few more of the texts you've used, whether you've created them or they've been downloaded. Record them all on your reading level tracking sheet (Appendix A) and look at the range. Has your class had a suitable range? We'll talk more about that in Chapter 8.

THE TAKEAWAY

So, you've seen how the different analysis systems work and how things like word complexity are so important when calculating an accurate reading level for your content. I began the chapter (after a brief history lesson) by asking why I would recommend different systems to the one that has been around the longest and is used the most widely. The answer is simple: you need something that works for the children in your class and word complexity is a big part of that, especially in a primary setting, and needs to be considered.

In the next chapter, I'll go into more detail about when you need to be assessing your content, whether it matters how often it is 'within range', and why.

8

HOW OFTEN SHOULD YOU BE CHECKING?

TEACHERS HAVE SPOKEN

I recently ran an online CPD session with several hundred teachers and I asked them a few questions about their habits when creating content for their class. Around 50 per cent of the teachers who responded said they create content for their class at least once a week. Over 75 per cent were creating content at least once a fortnight. That's great news; after all, one of the big messages in this book is that teacher-created content is going to be much more effective.

However, it wasn't all good news. I also asked what it was that teachers struggled with the most when creating their own content. A total of 32 per cent said that the main thing they struggled with was pitching their texts at the correct reading level – the joint most popular answer. So, considering that many teachers are attempting to create their own content but are struggling with the reading level, how important is it that every text *is* at the correct reading level?

IT'S NOT ABOUT ALL THE TIME

Despite how important it is that children are exposed to texts at the correct level, I firmly believe that it isn't important that *every* piece of content that they access is at the correct level. We'll talk more about genre in the next chapter, but there will be many cases where your content is at a lower reading level for legitimate reasons. There will also be cases where it's lower *just because it is*. That's also fine.

The one big exception to this is when texts are too high. Pitching a text slightly above a child's reading ability is good practice and helps them to progress, but if the text is too far above them, then it will quickly drift out of their zone of proximal development and you will end up with the issues discussed in Chapters 4 and 5.

What about their ZPD if it's too low? Good question! Repeatedly reading content that is too easy will definitely lead to boredom and children switching off. Some of that can be overcome by your amazingly interesting content, but it is also important to remember that too low is also often not a good thing either. Which leads us back to the question: how often should you be checking the reading level of your content?

In Teacher Task 6 (see Chapter 7), you started to record the reading levels of a few pieces of content on the appendix sheet (Appendix A). We are going to be using that a lot in this chapter because the simple answer is, I think you should be checking the reading level of most of your content.

SOMETIMES IT'S ABOUT KNOWING, NOT DOING

There's an important distinction between checking the reading level of your content and doing something about it. Once you've bookmarked the link to your favourite analyser (see Chapter 7), it will take you less than 30 seconds to analyse content once it is created, so it isn't really an onerous job. However, by doing so, you can easily do a few things.

TOO HIGH?

If you analyse a piece of content and it's too high, you can quickly alter it until it is at a more appropriate level (see Chapter 11 for tips on how to do this). This way, you know that you aren't wasting your prep time and possibly a lesson trying to get your class to work with a text that they can't comprehend. It's better to spend a few minutes now than a second lesson correcting it.

TOO LOW?

Is it time to worry about it being too low? Well, if you've spent that 30 seconds analysing each piece of content and you've recorded it on your appendix sheet, then you can make that judgement. This is where you might need to have a discussion with your English coordinator or members of your senior leadership team. How often your children should be exposed to correctly pitched content might come down to a whole-school decision. My recommendation would be roughly once a week or once a fortnight as a minimum.

CONTEXT IS KEY

Again, this will vary depending on what your long-term planning looks like. If you are working from the same model text for three weeks, then you're not going to be creating new content as often as somebody who uses a text for a week. You can look at this two ways:

It will be longer between texts, so my minimum period between correctly levelled texts will be longer.

Or:

> *I'm going to be using this text for three weeks; imagine how much exposure they'll get if it's correctly pitched.*

Neither of these choices is right or wrong, and they both depend on your own particular context. If the text is a particular genre (see Chapter 9), then it might necessarily be lower than you'd expect. That's fine, and to push it up would be a pointless waste of your time.

I made the point in Chapter 1 that the teacher-created content we are considering shouldn't be limited to English lessons. I'll repeat that here because it's important. If you've created a piece of content for a history lesson or a set of maths problems, analyse them and record the level. You might well find that your model text for English that you are going to use for three weeks is low, but that you used three other pieces of content across the curriculum that were at the correct level. (I agonised about using the word 'correct' here and considered using 'appropriate' instead, but neither are perfect. All it means is that they are within the reading band for the age of the children; as we've discussed, it's not always *correct* or *appropriate* for them to be at that level.)

All of this will also depend on your setting. Primary teachers will have different requirements and opportunities from teachers in secondary schools. If you are a secondary history teacher, for instance, your content might be refreshed more or less frequently, but will possibly be the only content they see in your subject. You might need to consider, in a different manner, when your content needs to be at that level, but keeping track in the same way as we've discussed will give you the information to make that decision.

WHAT DOES ALL THIS LOOK LIKE?

I like things to be crystal clear if I'm being asked to do something; it's just one of my many personality quirks. If somebody ever told me to mark books 'as often as you think it appropriate', it would annoy me to distraction, especially if that person was then going to judge or grade me on said marking. So I know that if I was in your shoes, reading this book, then I would want to know what all of this might look like in practice.

Let's consider an average week in a primary school. You will probably be teaching four or five English lessons, probably the same number of reading sessions, a couple of topic sessions covering either history or geography, a science lesson and maybe a few other bits and pieces. I've not included maths here because not all maths lessons will require content that falls under the remit of this book. That's probably in the region of 12–15 sessions where your children will be accessing your content in some form or another. Within that mix, there will almost certainly be the scope for one or two pieces to be pitched at the age-appropriate level for your class. It doesn't matter whether that comes in an English lesson or in science, whether it's a reading comprehension or a history information sheet.

Don't forget, the whole purpose of exposing your class to reading content at the correct level isn't to improve your English lessons or to improve their writing; those are just great side effects of the process. The main purpose is to make them better readers, and that can be done in any subject.

Giving your class these texts to read in a short space of time, as a speed-read activity first thing in the morning for instance, can help to ensure that your children are exposed to correctly levelled texts every single day.

BROADEN THE SPREAD

It's important to realise that all subjects are great opportunities to put correctly levelled texts in front of your class, but it's equally important to remember that children learn best when their curriculum is rich and varied. This is no different for your content and is another reason why it's important to keep track of as much of your levelled content as you can.

Speed reads are a great idea, but they shouldn't be the only exposure your children get. They should be used as reinforcement to an otherwise balanced spread. Consider them the ketchup on a varied reading diet. Likewise, the burden shouldn't always fall on English content, or science, or history, etc.

The appendix sheet (Appendix A) is only one way of tracking your analysed content; feel free to come up with your own that works for you and share it with me online. I'd love to see how you adapt it to suit your own context.

KNOWLEDGE IS POWER

However you choose to record it, this information should be the bedrock of the answer to the question – how often should your content be correctly levelled? You will begin to form a picture that highlights what the spread is in your classroom, whether you are relying on one subject too much or if you have a nice balance. Once you've got that, you will become more confident when you have a week with no content at the correct level at all, because you will know that the month before you had half a dozen pieces, or that in the following week you'll be looking at a correctly levelled piece all week in English.

WHAT ABOUT SECONDARY TEACHERS?

The same basic concepts apply whether you are in a primary or secondary setting. Your week will look different from a primary teacher's, but you will still be using content to teach your class. If you only teach a specific class once or twice a week, then it might be that your content needs to be correctly levelled more often, but you will likely be using it with more than one class.

It might be that you will be using your content for consecutive weeks, so your time spans between texts will be longer. However, the idea of balancing over your curriculum still holds true; you might just have fewer total opportunities to hit that reading level over a year. If you aim for half of your content to be correctly levelled, and the other subject teachers do the same, then the children in your school will be getting an excellently balanced and levelled reading curriculum.

TAKEAWAYS

This is an important chapter partly because the questions it addresses are some of the most frequently asked, but also because the idea behind it is one of the most important in the book.

The entirety of Part 1 was all about why it is critical for the children in your class to have access to correctly levelled text, so it's only fair that we consider how often that should happen. But it's equally important to remember that a broad range of texts at different levels is equally important.

So far, I haven't mentioned your workload in all of this, and there are two reasons for that. First, I think it's important to understand why I said 'once a week' at the beginning without worrying about how that will impact on workload. Hopefully, after seeing the breakdown of a week and recognising that there is a wide range of content that can be included, you are panicking less about that.

Second, Chapter 10 goes into lots of detail about how to raise or lower the reading level of your text and, by the time you've finished reading that and had a little bit of practice, the impact on your workload should be minimal. Not only that, once you've done it a few times, you will start to write at the correct level naturally and you won't need to change much at all.

Now that we know how often we need to check the level of our content (as often as possible) and how often we need to worry about it (once a week unless it's too high), we can move on to look at why it might be okay for it to fall outside the age range and what might cause it.

9

WHY MIGHT CONTENT BE OUT OF RANGE?

I mentioned in Chapter 8 that there's no need for all your texts to be at the age-specific level for your class. We covered how often you should be aiming to achieve that, but I thought it would be beneficial to show you where and why there might be cases that the text is lower or higher than you would like.

The same caveat still applies as in the previous chapter; if your text is too high, then that's something to concern yourself with. You can use the tips and guidance in Chapter 11 to help with that. This chapter will look at some reasons why it might be too high and the rare occasions where that might be something you can choose to accept.

Why, then, might a text be too low?

GENRE

Read the following sentence and think about what it's trying to achieve and where it might be appropriately taught.

It was dark. Hana could sense her pupils widening, but it was no good. Frost bit at her cheeks. Snow fell in towering drifts. Something watched. Something in the darkness. She ran. She stumbled on a gravestone but steadied herself. It was close; she could tell just by the sound of its breath. It leapt.

What do you think? For me, the intent is clear (perhaps because I wrote it), but the purpose of the text is to build tension. One of the main ways to do that, indeed one of the success criteria that most teachers will give to children to achieve this, is to use short, sharp sentences and short vocabulary.

When I say short vocabulary, I am, of course, referring back to syllables. It's nearly always more effective in tense narratives to use language that is quicker to say. It's probably always going to be more effective to say the potion 'bubbled' than to say it was 'effervescent', as much as the latter is more evocative. If you were writing an adventure story, or slowly describing a mad scientist's laboratory, then effervescent might well be the better choice.

We know that sentence length and vocabulary choice play a significant role in calculating a reading level, so it makes sense that shorter, sharper texts will have a lower level. In fact, the text above has a reading level of low Year 2.

However, despite the low reading level, the content, imagery and style, not to mention the punctuation, indicate that it's probably an Upper Key Stage 2 text. Should a teacher who wrote this be worrying and spending time trying to get it to a level closer to Year 6? Not at all. You would completely destroy the impact you were setting out to achieve.

A lot of this comes down to the ideas we will discuss in Chapter 13 when we look at the purpose of a text. It's important to remember that you, as a teacher, are ultimately the guiding light with these matters. Neither I nor this book are here to tell you what to do. The text above is a great example of building tension and it will hook the children. As long as I know that it is low, I can make sure that other content I create is higher. It's all about keeping track and making informed decisions.

Just as an exercise to prove my point, I've rewritten the paragraph using the tips in Chapter 10. I think you'll agree that it loses some of its impact, even though it is still a good piece of descriptive writing.

> *It was dark, pitch black and filled with even darker shadows. Hana brushed her hair from her cheek, blinked and started to sense her pupils widening, but it was no good. Ice-cold frost bit at her cheeks, causing them to turn red and an involuntary shiver to scurry along her spine. Pillowy white snow floated slowly to the ground, gathering in towering drifts. Something watched Hana from the darkness; she could sense its eyes boring into her soul. She ran forwards, hoping to get away from whatever had decided to make her its prey. A gravestone reared up out of the ground like a garish prop in a haunted mansion and snatched at her legs, causing her to stumble. She steadied herself by throwing her arms out wide, but she cursed at the lack of light. Whatever was following her was close now; she could tell by the rasping, hissing sound of its rotten breath that filled her lungs with every step she took. With a suddenness that surprised her, the creature leapt and tumbled to the ground with its arms around her neck.*

It may even work as a piece of tense writing, but if the device that I want my children to focus on is short sentences, then putting that in front of them will have no impact. In fact, it will probably encourage the opposite. All of that and it *still* only has a reading level of Year 4.

ESSENTIAL LANGUAGE

The bubonic plague. You've no doubt heard about it, you might even have taught it, but it's got a pretty tricky name. Imagine a piece of content that you've created to give children in your class information about this most terrible of diseases. You're probably going to include words like 'microbe', 'microorganism', 'bubo', 'pestilence', 'pandemic', 'epidemic', 'dysentery', 'noxious', 'culprit', and so on.

If you think back to where the weighting was given by the analysers, a lot was placed on the commonality of vocabulary in the text. These are not words that will appear very often outside this context. Some will be more common than others, but they will all score quite highly. This is the same with lots of topic-specific language.

We discussed contextual knowledge in Chapter 7 when we discussed a child who has read a lot about dinosaurs. By the end of your topic on plague, the children will definitely know most, if not all, of those words and be able to comprehend them accordingly. At the beginning of the topic, you will probably put things in place to help them, whether that's a key vocabulary sheet or a display. However, the system doesn't know any of that, so it scores the text accordingly.

If you level a text and it's marginally high, then you have two choices (if it's more than a year too high, then it's unlikely that the vocabulary is entirely responsible).

Option one is to accept that it's close to the year group and the fact that it contains lots of topic vocabulary is to blame. Only you can make this choice. If it's a bit high, but you know there is only one topic-specific word, then it's probably a good idea to look a bit deeper.

Option two is my preferred option. It takes a few minutes, but is worth it. If you go through your text and replace the topic vocabulary with more common words, then relevel, you can see whether they were the issue or not. For instance:

> *Plague victims often suffered from pestilent buboes. The epidemic had spread across London by the end of September. At the time, doctors weren't aware of microbes or bacteria; they didn't really know the cause at all.*

This text has a reading age of middle Year 5. If this was for a Year 4 class, we would normally treat it as being too high. If we change some of the vocabulary, we can see a difference in reading age.

> *Plague victims often suffered from* rotten spots. *The* disease *had spread across London by the end of September. At the time, doctors weren't aware of* viruses *or* germs; *they didn't really know the cause at all.*

Suddenly, it has a reading age of middle Year 2 or low Year 3. In this instance, then, we can see that the use of 'pestilent', 'buboes', 'epidemic', 'microbes' and 'bacteria' were pushing the reading level up by almost two years.

There's an important point here that links back to my assertion that a text more than one year above is probably not entirely down to vocabulary. The impact of changing those words is more pronounced here than it usually would because the text is so short, so the average scores have more of an impact. Over a longer text, the impact would be less noticeable.

TEACHER JUDGEMENT

This isn't to say that you should blindly accept a higher level text just because it is topic-specific vocabulary that is causing it. Every time a child encounters a word that they don't recognise, it adds to their cognitive load. Not only is it another thing they need to work through before they can comprehend the text, it's also a blocker in the text. They have to stop reading, however momentarily, to work out what the word means.

If the words are critical to the understanding of the text, or if they are only a few in number, then this is perfectly fine. After all, they can only build up that understanding of vocabulary by being exposed to it. The balance between what is essential and what isn't, needs to be made by the teacher.

Let's look again at the first text.

Plague victims often suffered from pestilent buboes. The epidemic had spread across London by the end of September. At the time, doctors weren't aware of microbes or bacteria; they didn't really know the cause at all.

Just by removing the words 'pestilent' and 'microbes', the reading level drops to low Year 5 or middle Year 4. I'd argue that they probably aren't essential in that text. 'Buboes' is a very specific word for this topic, so it is essential. 'Epidemic' is a good word to be exposed to, although it probably isn't essential.

So, there are times when the reading level might be high, but you choose to use it. Only you can make the decision about how much language is acceptable to include at once. It might be that you decide to spread the language out over a few texts. That way, they still get the exposure, but the cognitive load is spread out.

These are just a couple of times when you might find that your content is lower or higher than you would like, but when you might choose to use them anyway. Once you've completed the tasks in Chapters 10 and 11, you should have a much better understanding of how to adjust your reading levels accordingly.

Speaking of which, that's where we're heading next. We'll start by looking at how to increase the reading level when you aren't happy with it being too low.

10

HOW TO INCREASE THE READING LEVEL

In Chapter 9, we looked at why your content might have too high or too low a reading level and the situations where that might be acceptable. In most instances, though, you are probably going to want to do something about that. These next two chapters will guide you through what to look out for when you need to shift the level one way or another.

Hopefully, once you have gone through these exercises a few times with your own content, you will begin to recognise what to look out for as you write, which will save you even more time. Having said that, editing your level up or down shouldn't be a time-consuming exercise. Most of these tips, tricks and bits of advice should be quick to implement.

Once you've read Chapter 13, you will be able to see the link between focusing on the purpose of a text and how that can help you to change the reading level as well. For now, let's look at the important question: what will shift that level up?

WHAT MATTERS?

We covered how the reading levels are calculated extensively in Chapter 7, but it's worth recapping the main points here because they are relevant to what we are about to do.

SENTENCE LENGTH

Sentence length is one of the most important factors in calculating a reading level and with good cause. Research suggests (Cowan, 2010) that children and young adults can retain between 3 and 5 pieces of information at any one time. This working memory is essential for reading comprehension at a sentence level, as well as on a broader text-wide level.

Perhaps more interestingly, the same research found that this memory storage was even lower if the participants didn't know when the information was going to end. For instance, if people were asked to memorise a list of numbers or objects given to them verbally, they remembered fewer than if they were written in front of them. The theory behind this is that the working memory is constantly updating and trying to remember more each time, with no knowledge of when it will end.

Younger readers, in particular, don't tend to scan a sentence, so they won't register when it is coming to an end. This has the potential to further reduce the working memory space when reading. This will become more important in the next chapter, but is worth bearing in mind now because it will impact the work you do here.

Knowing all of this, we can use it to our advantage to increase the reading level of a text. Read the following paragraph, with a reading level of Year 2.

The old man walked along the street. Trees hummed in the gentle breeze. Leaves drifted to the ground. Around him, the world seemed to carry on regardless of the deep sadness that washed over him. He took his usual seat on an old bench. He cried softly, brushing his hand over a metal plaque. Only the most observant passer-by would have been able to read the name of his wife etched into the silver.

The sentences are short and to the point, but they don't necessarily need to be. This is where Chapter 13 and knowing the purpose of your text is essential. If you are looking to use that particular technique, as we discussed in Chapter 9, then it would be fine to leave it as it is. But, if sentence length isn't something that you need your class to consider for this particular text, then it's easy to use that to increase the level.

Consider the following:

*The old man walked along the street **while** trees hummed in the gentle breeze. Leaves drifted to the ground **as, all around,** the world seemed to carry on regardless of the deep sadness that washed over him. He took his usual seat on an old bench **and** cried softly, brushing his hand over a metal plaque. Only the most observant passer-by would have been able to read the name of his wife etched into the silver.*

By using conjunctions to join shorter clauses together, it increases the reading level to Year 3. Over a longer text, doing this would increase it even further.

It's vital to understand that we aren't just doing this as a box-ticking exercise. It isn't something to do just so that we can say the text is at the right level. It has multiple purposes. In this case, not only is the text now at a reading level that might challenge the class or place it in their zone of proximal development, but it is also teaching them appropriate ways to join clauses and the impact this can have on the reader. I have joined them together quickly to make an example for this book, but you can use this as an opportunity to plug any gaps in this area if needed.

VOCABULARY CHOICE

We talked about word 'commonality' in Chapter 9, and it's another tool that we can use to increase the reading level of a text. You might choose to use this route when you want to increase the reading level slightly, but your sentence structure is key to your teaching goals.

In that case, you might not want to mess around with sentence length or structure. If so, look at your word choices. This can be a great opportunity to expand the vocabulary of your class, but as before, make sure that it is purposeful. Using less common words just to boost the reading level will be counterproductive, but using them with consideration to the text can be very effective.

For example:

> *Down by the slow, overflowing river, a young girl stood on the edge of an old bridge. A small lure, tied carefully to a thin thread, broke the water's surface. The girl's eyes didn't move from that tiny red dot – it was as if looking away would break some kind of spell.*
> (Reading age: Year 2)

The narrative is fine; the sentence structure adds to the text, so let's look at the vocabulary. If we attack it with a thesaurus with no real regard for the flow of the text, we can really bump up the reading age.

> *Down by the sluggish, turgid river, a prepubescent adolescent perched on the rim of a derelict bridge. An insignificant lure, attached prudently to a thin thread, penetrated the water's surface. The girl's eyes didn't stray from that minuscule scarlet dot – it was as if looking away would destroy some kind of enchantment.*

Suddenly, it has a reading age of Year 5, but does that mean it's a better text to give to a Year 5 class? Probably not. It doesn't really make sense in the same way and some of the easy flow of the text has been lost. To use this would be counterproductive and pointless. Instead, we can find a mid-ground.

> *Down by the slow, **swollen** river, a young girl stood on the edge of a **derelict** bridge. A small lure, tied carefully to a thin thread, broke the water's surface. The girl's eyes didn't **stray** from that tiny red dot – it was as if looking away would break some kind of spell.*

Just by changing three words, we can push the text up to a Year 4 level. That might be enough for what you need – it really depends on what year group you are aiming for. The point is, it doesn't often require wholesale changes to the vocabulary to increase the reading level. If you wanted to push it slightly higher still, you could supplement the vocabulary changes by joining two sentences together:

> *Down by the slow, swollen river, a young girl stood on the edge of a derelict bridge. A small lure, tied carefully to a thin thread, broke the water's surface, **but** the girl's eyes didn't stray from that tiny red dot – it was as if looking away would break some kind of spell.*

SENTENCE STRUCTURE

Think back to what we discussed at the beginning of Part 2 and how working memory links to reading levels. If I asked you to remember a logical sequence of things, whether that's numbers, letters or animals ordered by size, it would be easier for you to remember more of them than if I gave you a random sequence.

For instance:

62, 72, 82, 92, 102, 112, 122, 132, 142, 152, etc.

would be easier to remember than:

126, 642, 12, 90, 45, 5.2, 89, 4,021, etc.

When things are in a logical order, it's easier to process that information. We know this from our own experiences. You might find that you create a mental shopping list in the order that you will encounter the items in the store. If I asked you to name every child in your class, you might visualise your classroom layout and read off the children as you mentally move from chair to chair or you'll give them to me in register order. We like sequences.

Let's apply that to reading comprehension. Read the following sentence and visualise it at the same time.

A man walked down the street, looking ahead to the tall mountains that were covered in snow.

Things happen in the sentence in the order that they would happen in real life. The first thing the man would do is walk down the street. Only when he is doing that is he able to look ahead. Only when he is looking ahead is he able to see the mountains and only once he can see them does he know that they are covered in snow. Walking, looking, seeing mountains, snow. They are presented in the sentence in that order. That is an easier sentence to read because of it. There is less load on the working memory because very little needs to be remembered for the rest to make sense.

Try to do the same with this sentence. Think about what the very first image is that forms in your head.

Staring into the demonic, lifelike eyes of the twisted alien, the young boy turned off his computer, shuddered and vowed never to play the game again.

In this sentence, we've moved important information to the beginning. I would imagine that one of the first images you had was of somebody staring at an alien (I'll leave how twisted it was to your imagination). When you then proceed to the next clause, where the boy turns off his computer, you now need to remember what it was he saw; otherwise, the shuddering and vowing to never play the game don't make sense.

In the limited working memory of a child, if that first part of the sentence is lost, then you end up with:

The young boy turned off his computer, shuddered and vowed never to play the game again.

As a sentence, it's structurally fine, but it doesn't offer any information. If the reader is then asked *why* the boy vowed never to play the game again, they wouldn't be able to answer it.

Obviously, this isn't to say that you should never vary the structure of your sentences. Particularly in Key Stage 2, this is an important technique that your class needs to be exposed to and to learn. However, it is an important thing to consider when you are looking to shift the reading level of your content.

Just as with the word complexity, it doesn't take many sentence structure changes to make a big difference. Often, one or two is enough to raise a text by a whole year group.

TEACHER TASK 7

The text below has a reading level of lower Year 2. Using the tips in this chapter and your favoured reading level analyser, see if you can edit it to raise the reading level, first to Year 4 and then to Year 6. If you overshoot the first time, that's great. You can investigate why, or you can use the tips in the next chapter to lower it. Remember, the more you do this, the more natural it will become, and you'll find yourself doing it as you write.

A man lived alone underneath an old stone bridge. He was younger than you might think. His only possessions were a small red handkerchief and a battered crown. He kept them close by no matter where he went.

There was a dusty road that ran across the bridge. It ran for miles before stopping at the wall of a large castle. Big granite blocks rose from the dirt and stopped anybody from entering. The king didn't want any visitors. H had lived alone ever since his queen had died and his son had run away.

What did you find easiest to change? You might have used a mixture of all three points or focused on one. There's no right or wrong way of doing this; ultimately, you know your class, and you know what they need most. If they are struggling with complex sentences, then that might be the best place to focus on to increase the reading level. You will be achieving two goals with one text. The same goes for classes that struggle with vocabulary or reading stamina. As I've mentioned before, all of this is just another arrow in your quiver of information. How you use it is really down to you.

Moving on into Chapter 11, we will look at what to look at if you have the opposite problem. It might not surprise you to know that some of the advice is very similar to this chapter, but there are other things to consider as well, so do stick around.

11

HOW TO REDUCE THE READING LEVEL

Now that you know how to increase the reading level, reducing it is pretty much a case of reversing your thinking. However, there are some other things to bear in mind.

PURPOSE

When you are lowering the level of content, it's perhaps more important to keep in mind the purpose of the text than it was when you were raising the level. There is probably a reason why the reading level is high in your content, and it's probably down to something that you've included because you want your class to learn from it. If you remove that wholesale, then you are likely to end up with a text that isn't fit for purpose. This is why it's critical to really focus in on the purpose of your text before you write it. That way, you can make adjustments that won't impact it.

When I'm trying to reduce the reading level of my own content, I tend to work through it in the following order, always considering the purpose and style of the text.

STEP 1: SENTENCE LENGTH

As we explored in Chapter 10, sentence length is rightly one of the more important factors in calculating a reading level. In my experience of writing and levelling texts, this is where I most often overshoot and would always be my first port of call if I'm looking to reduce the reading level of a text.

If you are writing 500 words of content, then you have a lot of scope to play around with sentence length. That's a good thing, because it means that you can still use complex sentences, but also that there is enough content there to break some up into simple sentences as well.

One of the easiest ways to do this is to search your content for the word 'and'. If you're anything like me, your first drafts will be filled with sentences joined by 'and' or 'but'. A very easy way to reduce your reading level is to look at each use of 'and' and see if it's necessary (see what I did there?).

For instance:

It was a cold and stormy night, and the wind howled through the trees.

That second 'and' isn't really needed.

It was a cold and stormy night. The wind howled through the trees.

Think about the second option from a working memory point of view. In the first sentence, there are three things to remember (cold, stormy and the fact that it is night). In the second, there are two (wind and trees). Both of those are well within that 3–5 working memory slots that we discussed in Chapter 10. In the first option, all five things are in one sentence. That's a lot for a child to keep in their working memory. The pause between the sentences also gives the reader time to stop and process what they've just read.

STEP 2: WORD IMPORTANCE

We've looked at how word commonality is important when it comes to reading level (see Chapter 7), so it's always a good idea to assess any high-level language for how critical it is to the text. If you use the paid Lexile® system, it will give you a list of words that are impacting the level (the ATOS system doesn't have anything similar, but it's up to you whether that's worth paying for considering you still don't get a specific level with the paid Lexile system).

I talked about the impact that topic-specific vocabulary can have in Chapter 9, and it bears thinking about here as well. If your reading level is too high, look at the vocabulary you have used. Try the tips in Chapter 9 to decide whether it is only the topic-specific vocabulary that is impacting it.

This is where your teacher judgement will come into play. You will know what other content your children have been or are going to be exposed to. Using the example of a geography topic looking at rivers, the children will eventually need to know words such as 'sediment', 'oxbow', 'erosion', 'basin', 'abrasion', 'confluence', 'irrigation', and so on. If you include all of those in one text, then the reading level will sky rocket.

Look at your unit plan and think about where they are absolutely needed. You might find that some of them aren't needed for a few weeks, so they can be introduced one at a time. Likewise, if the content you are levelling is for the end of the unit, then there is a good chance that they will already have been exposed to those words and will know them, so you can use the tips in Chapter 9 to ignore them and get a reading level for the rest of the text.

Adjusting the vocabulary – in fact, adjusting any part of the content – is a juggling act. On one hand, they need to know the vocabulary and your class won't learn them without being exposed to them. On the other hand, they *are* tricky, context-specific words, and this means that they do make a text harder to read and *will* make it less comprehensible. Drip feeding this kind of language through several texts is the best way to achieve this balance for your entire class.

Don't forget to utilise other content as well. You may not be able to get 'erosion' into your first geography lesson, but if you are creating content for your reading comprehension sessions, why not include it there? You could even link it to a question so that you can assess your class's understanding of these key words.

STEP 3: SENTENCE STRUCTURE

If you've read Chapter 10, then you'll know that I've already discussed sentence structure and its impact on reading levels in depth. It is one of the most common things I notice in my own writing when I'm looking to reduce the reading level, so it's definitely something to consider here as well.

If you remember from Chapter 10, the average child can retain 3–5 pieces of information in their working memory, and this is helped if the pieces of information are in a logical order.

You've probably seen the endless discussion online about fronted adverbials and what they are and so on, but this is the point where I'd recommend you start looking out for them. This is especially important for children below Year 4 when they are first introduced to fronted adverbials on the curriculum.

Afterwards, we all went to John's for a party.

If we analyse this sentence, there are two points where the working memory is required to memorise information outside a logical order.

First, the reader has to remember, for the entire sentence, that whatever they are about to read is happening *afterwards*. (We can assume that there was an event that took place just before the sentence.) Then, they are required to remember that whatever happens afterwards is going to happen at John's. It's only at the end that we get to the point of the sentence – the party.

If we rewrite it in a more logical order, we get:

We all went for a party at John's afterwards.

The order of what they are doing, where they are doing it and when, is more logical and so, over a longer text, would have a lower reading level.

TEACHER TASK 8

In a similar vein to Teacher Task 7, you will be using the information in this chapter to reduce the reading level of the follow text. Instead of asking you to reach a certain level, I'm going to ask you to play around with the different techniques I've introduced above and see what impact they have. Try to keep the same general feel and idea, if you can. In my experience, it is much harder to reduce a level and keep these things consistent than it is to raise them.

This original text has a reading level of Year 5:

> *While all of us were jubilant, elated even, to see Meghan again, we were some-what nonplussed by her ragged appearance, probably a direct result of her brief skirmish with the wild pack of wolves that roam our street at night. Nonetheless, the others all rushed over to hug her and pat her on the back in some sort of primal ritual, like mother hens pecking at their solitary chick.*
>
> *In a way, it's strange, I suppose, that I've never really understood all of those obscure things that gangs and groups do when they celebrate, especially given the fact that my dad was a professional football player and often celebrated with preposterous handshakes, backslaps and other theatrical nonsense. Perhaps that's why I always feel like an outsider, an interloper into a strange scene in a stranger play, whenever these things occur.*
>
> *Just as I started to feel awkward, like a weakened gazelle on the edge of the herd, Meghan broke free of their embrace and rushed over to me. She launched into a hug of her own, threatening to break my already bruised ribs, and gave me one of her brightest smiles. 'I know you're glad to see me, really,' she said and punched me on the arm.*
>
> *I grunted some sort of non-committal reply. In truth, I suppose I was glad to see her. She was one of my closest friends and my only confidant; she knew more about me than anybody else. I guess I just wasn't sure I was ready to forgive her, to move on from the betrayal that I felt the moment she launched herself from the helicopter and plummeted headfirst into the swirling mael-strom below.*

IN SUMMARY

That brings us nicely to the end of Part 2. You've seen what a reading level is and how it's calculated. Hopefully, this has given you an insight into how to adjust your own content to better meet the needs of your class. I've shown you why the level might justifiably be too high or too low and what to do about it if you want to adjust it either way.

Ultimately, the decisions on how to use this information will come from you as a teacher. You know your class and your past, and future outcomes for them. As with everything in this book, this information is just that, information. Definitely bear in mind what I said about the need for genre and style to have an equal importance. If you are using tense writing that packs a punch with a lower reading level, embrace it and use it, but keep it in mind so that you can raise the reading level bar next time.

It's also important to recognise that we are doing all of this to improve the reading levels of the children in our care and to make sure that they can access the content that we create. It isn't intended to be a tick-box exercise just to say we've done it. It's perfectly acceptable to look at a piece of content and know that it is only high because of the topic-specific vocabulary, but that higher level will still have an impact on the children's comprehension, regardless of the reason behind it. Only you can decide whether they have had enough exposure to the language already to overcome that, or whether the word choice is essential for that text.

In the third and final part of the book, I'll show you how to do everything we've discussed in Parts 1 and 2 while saving time. If you're a subject coordinator or a senior leader, there are also some great ideas for ensuring a consistent approach across the entire school.

PART 3

TEACH IT: WHAT CAN YOU DO TO SAVE TIME AND INCREASE THE EFFECTIVENESS OF YOUR CONTENT?

12

THE IMPORTANCE OF BALANCE AND SAVING TIME

Teachers spend a lot of time preparing for lessons. On average, primary teachers spend around 7.8 hours a week prepping and secondary teachers spend around 7.3 hours (Walker et al., 2019). That's a lot of time, so it's important that any work carried out in the name of planning is efficient and gets maximum results.

Part 3 of this book is all about tackling a part of your planning. We've established that you should be creating as much of your own content as possible and that you should be considering the reading level that it is written at. Now, we are going to look at how you can do all of that without having a negative impact on your workload.

In this chapter, we will also look at why it is important for your class that your content isn't taking you hours to create.

THINK ABOUT THE OUTCOME

Let's consider a typical English unit of work that relies on a model text. At the beginning of the unit, you will present your class with a text. It might be a 500-word story or a piece of non-fiction. You might get them to internalise the text over the next few days. At some point, you will break down the text into the components that you are hoping your class will learn. These might be grammar objectives, structural objectives or something else entirely.

By the end of the unit, you will quite probably have an innovation period, culminating in the class writing their own, innovated version of the original text you gave them. You will probably give them around 45 minutes to write it. So, in this heavily simplified world, your class of children, whether they are 6 years old or 14 years old, will have 45 minutes to create their own text based on a set of criteria that you have given them. Think back to when you wrote that text. If, like 69 per cent of respondents to my survey, you are taking at least an hour to write your own version of that text, what hope have your class got of doing it in less time? The answer to this isn't to give your class longer to write; it's to look at why it is taking you so long to write the text in the first place. The average typing speed is around 40 words per minute, which means that a 500-word document should take a little over 12 minutes to type up. The rest of the time is spent working out what to type.

Part of learning how to create content quicker will be to look at your own process and work out what is taking you the most time. Generally, these time vacuums will be one of the following areas.

IDEAS

Writing creatively isn't easy. I have always felt that there is this expectation that teachers, particularly primary school teachers, must all be great creative writers. Perhaps it's because so many children's authors were once teachers, or maybe it's because teachers are often very good at talking creatively within their lessons. It wouldn't be unusual to visit a secondary school science lesson and see the teacher finding creative ways to memorise key chemical formulas or a maths teacher singing and dancing their way through algebra. Teachers are a creative bunch, but that doesn't necessarily link directly to creative writing.

We'll look in more detail at some ideas that will reduce this burden in Chapters 16–21, but it's important to remember that it's absolutely okay to struggle with coming up with ideas for your content. I've written over a thousand short reading comprehensions for The Literacy Shed and a large handful of children's books, and there are still days when I'm banging my head against my desk trying to figure out what to write about next.

It's also important to remember that the lessons you are teaching are English language lessons. They aren't creative writing workshops. While your writing needs to be engaging, it doesn't need to stand the test of time like a literary classic. We'll cover this idea more in Chapter 13. In my survey, 31 per cent of teachers said that struggling to come up with ideas was their biggest hurdle, so you are far from being alone if you fall into this category.

OBJECTIVES

I've seen many teachers struggle with this subject – if it's your pitfall, you're not alone. This is such a big issue that the whole of Chapter 13 is dedicated to dealing with it. By objectives, I mean struggling to work out what needs to be included in the text and what can be left out. Once again, 31 per cent of teachers said that this was their biggest hurdle when creating content, so you are in good company.

REACHING EVERYONE

This subject ties in with the overall theme of this book, in that reading level is a big part of making sure that your text is accessible to your whole class, but it also spreads its devilish wings wider than that. Teachers in my survey were able to give an open-ended answer to this question and I found that many of them could be grouped under this same umbrella. A few of the responses I received were (I've shortened them where necessary):

- Ensuring that all features are included without losing the flow.
- In a large class, it is challenging to write a text that all children can access – it may not have high enough vocabulary or reading level to challenge or be too difficult for others.
- Writing things that all children can access but that are still relevant.

When I look at those responses, all I can think about is the purpose of the text. While there will always be a range of reading levels across a class, particularly a mixed-year group class, everything else should be more or less the same. If you are writing content to inform the class about the causes of the Second World War, it doesn't matter their reading level; they all need the same information.

Again, we will cover this in a lot more detail in Chapter 13, but it's worth considering that if you think your time vacuum falls into this category, you might actually be suffering from a case of objective-itis instead.

READING LEVEL

Hopefully, by now, you will know exactly how to deal with this issue from Part 2 of this book. It can be tricky to nail that reading level when you first start. I've been doing it for years and I still produce the odd text that is way outside of the range I was aiming for. But the more you do it and the more you evaluate and analyse your own content, the quicker and more natural it will become.

TEACHER TASK 9

Look at the last few pieces of content you created for your class. You can also do this task as you are creating a new piece of content; some people might find it easier that way. Whatever works best for you, you just need to be able to answer a few simple questions about it.

Probably the most important place to start is to think about how long the piece took you to create. Once you have been through the exercises in this book, I would hope that a 500-word text should take you no more than around 20 minutes to complete. This might be slightly longer if you have to research certain pieces of information for a topic-based information text, but see the notes on this in Chapter 13.

Are you happy with how long it took you to create? Think now about what it was that took most of the time. Where do you fit in the four categories above? It might be that

(Continued)

you are struggling with bits from all of the categories – many teachers do. That's not something to be worried about. None of this is a judgement on you as a teacher. Great teachers aren't those who can create perfect content easily and quickly; it just means that one part of their job is less time-consuming, and that's where I intend to get you by the end of this journey.

If you can get your hands on a range of content across several different subjects, then it's even more interesting to analyse. Do you struggle with the same areas in all subjects? Or is it the objectives holding you up in English but researching topic information in geography?

This is a great activity to do with other teachers in your school. If the time vacuums are broadly the same across the school, then it's a great opportunity to put some CPD into place to help everyone out. Think of the time savings across your school!

Now that you've identified some of your time vacuums, we can move on and start to look at how we can reduce their impact and increase your productivity. In Chapter 13, we are going to explore one of my favourite words when it comes to creating teaching content, and that's 'purpose'. It's so important that I use it three times in the chapter heading.

13

PURPOSE, PURPOSE, PURPOSE

When I talk to teachers about saving time when creating content, the word 'purpose' is one that I keep coming back to. In fact, I think it's such an important word that I've included it in the chapter title three times. I'll probably mention it dozens more times during the chapter as well. Purpose. Remember it! But why am I going to keep banging on about it?

Really, the importance of purpose is twofold. It's critical to really zoom in on the purpose of your content if you want to have any hope of writing it in a reasonable time. Not only that, if you aren't clear of the purpose, then the children in your class won't be.

I think it's time for another tale from my own classroom. I remember once writing a text for my Year 5 class. If memory serves (and that's less reliable than it once was), it was a text linked to the short film *The Piano*. I wasn't long out of my NQT weaning phase and I remember wanting to make sure that my content 'ticked all the boxes'. I've added the inverted commas there to highlight how I was feeling. I imagine you've probably had similar thoughts at some point.

Now, I've been to sleep too many times since then and far too much dust has settled in the caverns of my mind to remember how successful or not the lessons were based on the text. In fact, the only reason I remembered it was because I searched through all my older teaching folders for content that I'd created as research for this book. But, as soon as I read it, I remembered stressing about writing it.

In the dark recesses of my mind, I remember agonising over making sure I'd included as much of the punctuation they needed in Year 5 as possible, worrying about whether I'd included enough imagery and metaphorical language – ultimately, about whether or not it would cover everything that I felt it needed to. Ironically, one of the few things I didn't even consider was the reading level. I don't think many teachers I knew at the time did.

The long and short of it is that it took me a lot longer to write and caused more stress and anxiety than it needed to.

WHAT'S THE POINT?

The overall theme of this chapter can really be summed up in those three (or four if you don't contract) words.

We started this book by looking at all the different subjects that you might create content for. Now is a good time to revisit that because it's important. Which subject you are creating content for will have an impact on its purpose. If you are a secondary teacher and teach a single subject, within that, there will be other areas – sub-subjects, if you will. These will impact the purpose as well.

I believe that there are four overarching purposes for content in your classroom. The main three are:

- providing information;
- meeting a SPaG (spelling, punctuation and grammar) objective;
- providing structural scaffolding.

And then there's a fourth, less common purpose: asking a question.

Whenever you are creating a piece of content for your class, you should try to aim to meet one of those purposes, and that's it. At the absolute most, I'll allow you two if you promise not to tell anybody.

The easiest way to look at this is to imagine you are writing word problems for a maths lesson. The purpose there is simple: asking a question. You aren't likely to be trying to impart information on the French Revolution in a maths question. There's little chance that you will pose it in the form of a formal letter, and I doubt you'll be using it as a way of teaching passive voice. Those examples may be hyperbolic, but ask yourself why they seem so outlandish.

It wouldn't make any sense to do it, that's why.

The same holds true with content that you create for other areas of your teaching.

TEACHER TASK 10

Read the following short text and think about which of the three purposes I gave above it falls into.

The city of Pompeii became famous in 79 CE when its citizens were frozen in time. The nearby volcano, Mount Vesuvius, erupted somewhere around noon on the 24th of August. The ash and smoke that it shot into the air smothered the city, along with extremely hot gases. Most people were crushed or asphyxiated. It has been estimated that around 2,000 people died in the tragedy.

Where would you place it? The only purpose I focused on when I wrote it was to impart basic information about the eruption of Mount Vesuvius in 79 CE. There is very little imagery or creative language in there, no challenging grammar, and it is set out like a simple information text. Compare that with the following:

> *The infamous city of Pompeii grew in notoriety when it was suffocated in a ghostly pall of ash and dust. Despite their scurried attempts at fleeing the city, many civilians lost their lives when the grumbling Mount Vesuvius finally spewed forth its molten eruption.*

The focus here is very much on language and vocabulary. There is very little information given over. That doesn't make it a bad text; it just serves a different purpose. The first text might serve well in a geography or history lesson where the class is learning about Pompeii for the first time. They need to know the critical historical information to access the unit. The second text would work better in a reading comprehension lesson, perhaps when they already know the facts.

Remember our discussion about context-specific language? This is a good example of a text that would be either more or less accessible depending on the children's prior knowledge.

Now consider an amalgamation of both approaches.

> *In 79 CE, the infamous city of Pompeii found itself catapulted into notoriety when the nearby volcano, Mount Vesuvius, erupted. The cataclysmic event sent tons of ash and dust metres into the air; the unearthly shadows spawned panic and disarray in the city itself. Despite their frantic efforts to flee their impending zoom, over 2,000 souls perished in the tragedy.*

What did you notice most about it? What did you pick up on? Chances are, you will probably have focused on something slightly different from the next reader and different from myself. That's one of the big problems with a mish-mash of purposes. Imagine being a child reading that text. What would you take from it?

If you gave the class that text in your first history lesson, hoping that they'd take key factual information from it, can you guarantee that they won't be distracted by the language? Will they be able to decode the facts from the imagery? By confusing the purpose, you are making their job more difficult than it needs to be.

It's all well and good me telling you to think about each of these purposes, but how do they apply to your content in the context of your classroom?

PROVIDING INFORMATION

There are many cases where you will need to provide information to your class. The easiest examples are in so-called 'topic' lessons – geography, history and science, but it's also true for English and reading lessons. You might be presenting a character profile based on a character from a book or from your own imagination. Telling the reader what they look like, how they act, etc., is providing them with information.

In fact, I think these are the type of text where a lot of confusion can creep in around the purpose. It's very easy to slip into focusing on the language and vocabulary when you are describing somebody – to describe them as a towering hulk of a man, rather than just saying they were slightly over seven feet tall. But, if you want your children to know accurately and efficiently how tall the character is, which sentence will deliver that information most effectively?

Another factor to consider is how the information you are imparting affects the overall reading experience of the text. In Chapter 9, we considered the fact that some content might have a slightly higher reading level because of the context-specific language included in it. If you are going to include lots of this language, then the text really becomes about the vocabulary, not about the information.

If the reader has to use their cognitive load to process what words like 'magma', 'dormant', 'molten', 'conduit', 'fissure', and so on mean, they are less likely to comprehend or retain the date and death toll of the Pompeii disaster, for instance. This leads us nicely on to the next topic.

MEETING A SPAG OBJECTIVE

There will be plenty of times when you want to use a piece of content to demonstrate the use of fronted adverbial phrases, or the use of passive voice for impact, or the way in which rhetorical questions can draw the reader in. There will be times, as above, when you want your class to be exposed to key vocabulary (though remember the points in Chapter 9 about trying to spread these out to keep the reading level at an appropriate pitch). I lump all these under the banner of meeting a SPaG objective.

Even within this section, I have a hard-and-fast rule of focusing on no more than two elements of this purpose. That doesn't mean that you can't include other bits, but they shouldn't be your aim and you shouldn't be wasting time trying to fit them in. This purpose is probably one of the biggest time vacuums I have seen.

Think about the text I wrote for *The Piano*. I tried to include all the Year 5 grammar objectives in that one text. We are all guilty at times of doing something like this, of trying to expose the class to as many of the things they need to know as possible. It's a noble aim, but it's doomed to fail. All we are doing when we cram so many different things is dilute all of them. There becomes no clear purpose to the text because there isn't one. Instead, it's a jumbled mess of expectations.

But we can't exclude them all, either, otherwise the text becomes stilted and difficult to read. This is why I say limit yourself to two SPaG objectives (and only then if the SPaG purpose is your sole purpose for the text). Others can appear, but only if they happen naturally as you are writing it. For instance, if I wanted to focus on the following Year 6 grammar objectives:

- use of the passive voice,
- using semi-colons to mark boundaries between clauses,

they aren't naturally linked, but it may be that my grammar objective for the class last week was the use of semi-colons and I want to recap that while demonstrating this week's objective, using the passive voice.

I might use something like the following content (yours will probably be longer, but I've got a word count to stick to here).

*Some time around noon yesterday, a terrible crime **was committed** on the property of the Three Bears. When they returned home, after a long day working in the forest, Mr D. Bear discovered a scene of carnage; some of his descriptions were so horrific that we had to leave them out of the newspaper.*

*At first, only the living room seemed to have **been disturbed**. The porridge that they had left on the table had **been eaten**, and their rocking chairs **were destroyed.** On further investigation, Mr Bear discovered that their beds had **been disrupted by the criminal** as well!*

You can see that the semi-colon objective is demonstrated, but that I haven't gone over-board. If it was the objective last week, I want to revisit it, but I don't want to overuse it and take away from this week's objective. It also means that it's less for me to think about and therefore takes less time to write.

I've included passive voice five times (in bold) because this is my main objective and I want to show how it can be used in different ways.

Other than that, there are a few fronted adverbial phrases, one embedded clause, and that's it, really. They came naturally as I was writing the content; they weren't a conscious choice. There's no need to worry about anything else.

You'll notice that I've also kept the vocabulary at a reasonably challenging level for Year 6, but that I haven't introduced any new challenging vocabulary at this point. For instance, I could have changed 'committed' for 'perpetrated', 'working' for 'toiling' and 'horrific' for 'distressing'.

If this unit was focusing on newspaper writing, as the sample text suggests, then I would want to use another session to introduce the idea of sensationalist language. At that point, I might present them with the same text as above, but with the new language. That way, they are already familiar with the structure and the grammar objectives and they can focus on what I want them to – the vocabulary. I'll talk more about how you save time like this in Chapter 15.

STRUCTURAL SCAFFOLDING

In the example above, the text was based on a newspaper report. With many text types that you teach, you'll want to teach the children the structure of the text and why that particular type has that particular structure and what impact that has on the reader. For the purposes of this book, I'm referring to that as structural scaffolding. It's probably the texts where you will investigate the structure or create success criteria for the text.

For a formal letter, the structural scaffolding points might be:

- use of formal language;
- use of formal sentence starters;
- the structural order of the letter – who you are, why you are writing, what you hope to achieve, etc.;
- use of formal connectives;
- use of impersonal language;
- use of passive voice, etc.

Normally, I would say that you should focus on one or two of these criteria, but for structural scaffolding, it depends on the purpose of the text (I told you the word would crop up a lot).

If you are presenting the text to the class as a way for them to identify the criteria that you have highlighted, then it makes sense that the text should include all of them. In that case, your focus should be entirely on the scaffolding criteria – nothing else matters, not high-level vocabulary, not SPaG objectives (outside the scope of the success criteria) and, I would argue (and will do convincingly in Chapter 14), not the topic content.

However, if your focus is to demonstrate the accurate and detailed use of some of the criteria, then you need to rein yourself in and limit yourself to two of them at most. The same cognitive load issues still hold true here. If you really want your class to focus on and understand why the use of formal and impersonal language is important for a formal letter, then that is what you should be focusing on. Including lots of examples of the rest of the criteria will only muddy the water.

Obviously, I'm not saying that the rest of the content shouldn't follow the general structure of a formal letter – that would be odd and confusing – but they shouldn't be your focus when you are creating it. Passive voice might creep in where appropriate, but you shouldn't be spending your valuable time trying to force it in there if it doesn't fit naturally. There will be other content that you create during the unit that can include it. This is why it can be a good idea to link reading sessions to your English units; a selection of short formal letters for reading comprehension exercises could focus on different criteria each day.

TEACHER TASK 11

Pick out a selection of pieces of content that you have created for your class. They can be recent pieces or ones from the distant past if you'd prefer. If you can, it helps to do this activity without trying too hard to remember why you wrote it, so avoid any learning objectives, success criteria or other planning detritus attached to the content if you can. An alternative is to swap with a colleague from another year group who is familiar with the ideas in this book.

Read through each piece of content and see if you can work out which of the four purposes it was trying to fulfil. This might be difficult to do, especially if the author of the content wasn't clear in their own head when they created this. This isn't a bad thing – if you were creating perfectly purposed content already, you probably wouldn't be reading this part of the book.

Even after you've read this book and put it all into practice, it's still a great idea to revisit old texts and to try to decide where you need to focus moving forward. Remember, the point of figuring out the purpose is ultimately to save you time. It's not about being a good or bad teacher; it's about creating clear, concise content that is more effective and, therefore, a more efficient use of your time.

Once you've worked out what the purpose was (or not, if there wasn't a clear purpose), try to drill down further. If you think (or your colleague has told you) that the purpose was to impart information, try to work out what information that was. If it was a SPaG objective, which one you think it was.

When I tried this activity with the content I had created for our unit on *The Piano*, I couldn't work out any clear purpose at any level. It was quite clear that I'd tried to focus on everything.

If you want to graduate onto the masterclass level of this chapter, work through the content (with your colleague if it is theirs) and see what you could strip out or change to clarify the focus. This can be time-consuming, but it's a very effective way of stripping out one main purpose and then drilling down on the smaller purposes within it. It's a kaleidoscope of purposes, but there is one true purpose hidden within.

I started this chapter by telling you that I'd mention the word 'purpose' a lot – and I have. There are over 30 instances of the word in the chapter. That's because I honestly think that this is one of the cornerstones to achieving everything in this book in the most efficient way. For those of you who struggle to create content because it takes too long or because you find it hard to fit everything in, see this as a lifeline, a way out of the madness that drives you to spend hours on the same piece of content. Not only that, but hopefully now you can see how it will be more effective and more accessible for your class. That will not only save you time in the short term, but in the long term your class will absorb the information more quickly and retain it more easily, meaning that you have to spend less time covering areas again.

In the next chapter, we will look at linking your content to broader topics, why that might be costing you time and why it isn't always the best option for your class.

14

LINKING CONTENT TO A TOPIC AND WHY YOU MIGHT WANT TO RECONSIDER

Over the course of a school year, you might teach a dozen different topics. Whether they are the Ancient Greeks, space exploration or rivers and coasts, you will be creating content for a wide variety of different subject areas. Creating new and exciting content for each of these topics can be onerous and time-consuming, so how can we cut down on that time vacuum and work more efficiently?

I think it's only fair to pre-warn you that this chapter may contain ideas that you can't implement on your own – you might need to pass them up the chain and suggest school-wide changes. Your own context will be different from other people's and you may have the autonomy to implement some of the ideas, but you may not. When you get to the end of the chapter, think about how they might impact you and your colleagues, and have a professional discussion with your leadership team if you need to.

DOES TOPIC MATTER?

More importantly, does it matter if your teacher-created content fits in with the topic that you are teaching? To some, the idea that it might not be that important is sacrilege, so I can only apologise for the panic I might have caused you if that's the case. However, hear me out.

Thinking back to what you read in Chapter 13, the only time that I will concede that it is important to tie your content to your topic is if the purpose is to provide information. In that case, it would be ridiculous to suggest that a text designed to provide information about the American West should be written about the space race. Other than that, there are several solid reasons that I would recommend that it doesn't matter and, in fact, might be beneficial if your teacher-created content *doesn't* tie in with your broader class topic.

IT'S HARDER TO IMITATE

If the purpose of your text is to provide a scaffolding structure for your class, then tying it closely to the topic that they will be writing about can make it harder for them to innovate fully.

Let's assume that you are learning about Victorian England and your writing unit for the next week or so will be leading up to writing a formal letter home from a Victorian boarding school. You've already thought about the purpose of your content and narrowed it down to one; you are creating an example formal letter with the aim of providing a structural scaffold for what a formal letter should look like.

Here's where it gets a bit tricky for your children. There is only so much that can be written about from the point of view of a child trapped in a Victorian boarding school. When you present your letter to them, written from that point of view, the alternative directions that they can take can be quite limiting. The end result can often be that they cling quite closely to your own letter, changing the odd bit of vocabulary here or there, particularly the less confident writers.

If, however, your letter was a formal letter home from aboard the International Space Station, or the HMS *Beagle*, or even an alien planet, then your pupils will still get the same scaffolded support, but in a completely different context. Then, when they adapt it to their own content tied to the Victorian boarding school, everything is new and their own innovation.

It's not a decision that needs to be made for every single piece of content you write, but by having the freedom not to be tied to the specific topic that you are covering at that point in time will save you time when you're creating content and make it easier for your class to innovate from it.

TOPICS CHANGE

Particularly in primary education, topics often shift from one year to the next. You might make changes because of the curriculum, or as a school you might decide that a topic makes more sense in a different year group. Either way, you might spend a lot of time (though not too much, after reading this book) working on a brilliant model diary entry tied nicely to the Ancient Greeks, only to find that the following year you are teaching about the slave trade or the Amazon rainforest. If as a year group/school/academy chain, you had made the decision that your own model content didn't need to be linked to the topics, then your model diary would be just as useful the following year, and the one after, and so on.

THE MUDDYING OF THE PURPOSE

What is it that makes your content specifically linked to your topic? If you are creating a piece of content, whether it's a narrative, a diary entry or a newspaper report, what is it that links it to your topic? It's topic-specific vocabulary and content.

It might be the inclusion of Victorian paraphernalia – gas lamps, street urchins and the like – or the use of scientific language describing the International Space Station, but whatever it is, you are using content-specific flotsam to tie it in.

At that point, what stops the purpose of your text from shifting into the imparting of information? This is especially true for non-fiction text types. It's very difficult to focus on the structural scaffolding of a non-chronological report about bees if your model is also about bees. By the very nature of what you are creating, you will also be creating a text with the purpose of imparting information.

We know from Chapter 13 that this breaks the rules of purpose. The serious implication from Chapter 13 still holds true here, that you then run the risk of your class focusing on the wrong elements of the text, taking away information rather than the structure.

A much clearer way to approach this would be to have a piece of content created to impart the information that your pupils need about bees in a specific fact-finding lesson. That way, they can take information from multiple sources (there's nothing wrong with including a few pieces of third-party content alongside your own in these sessions; after all, you know that at least one of them is correctly levelled for their needs) and they don't need to focus on the structure.

Then, run a separate session with a different piece of content, focusing on the structure. For this content, it doesn't, and probably shouldn't, be anything to do with bees. This is a great opportunity to tie your content in with something that you know will grip your class. You could create it based on a book that you are reading in class and that you know you will probably read year on year.

If you do this, it will still be relevant next year, even if bees fly out the window, so to speak. You get the hook to draw the children's interest while allowing them to focus purely on the structure, which is the outcome for that particular piece of text.

LOCKED TO THE CONTEXT

I know when I started teaching, there was a common belief that I shared, that it was really important to fully immerse the class into a topic, and that if we could link everything we did to it, then that was only a good thing. I remember trying to link maths problems to obscure topics like the Aztecs, and so on. Since then, ideas such as a creative or a cross-curricular curriculum within schools have led to some teachers trying overly hard to make sure everything links. This can lead to forcing class reading texts into topics that they don't really suit, or worse, avoiding great books because they can't be linked to a topic. It also means that everything the children do during that unit is locked to that particular context.

In the example I gave above about a formal letter home from a Victorian boarding school, if the content you create is specifically tied to a Victorian boarding school, and they are linking everything they write to the Victorian period, perhaps entirely to the boarding school concept, and you are reading something like *Cogheart* (a fantastic book that begins with a pseudo-Victorian schoolgirl at a horrible boarding school and that absolutely should be read in schools), and then you are asking them to write their own formal letter based on the same limited concept, are they actually learning how to write a formal letter, or are they learning how to write a formal letter home from a Victorian boarding school?

If you asked them the following week to write a formal letter home from a soldier during the Second World War, would they be able to (assuming they had the relevant topic knowledge)? Or would they be limited because their entire contextual knowledge of formal letter writing is linked to a Victorian boarding school?

If, on the other hand, your scaffolding content had been a formal letter home from a stowaway aboard the *Beagle*, perhaps with a more positive bent than that which the children would ultimately innovate and write about, and your class text was something like *Nevermoor* (less Victorian but it still touches on the concept of being away from home), then their understanding of how different formal letters might look and their understanding of a broader range of emotions in that situation will be deeper.

TIME VACUUM

Ultimately, your time is precious and you have a lot of things to do. Do you really want to be creating the same text several times just to make it topic-specific? When you break it down, a diary entry is a diary entry, regardless of the specifics. A letter home from an Ancient Roman soldier will be structurally the same as one from a Victorian child at boarding school or a runaway aboard a pirate ship.

The thing that differentiates one from the other is the topic-specific fluff around the edges – the things that they have seen or heard or felt, etc. In other words, the stuff that might be important if your purpose is to give information but otherwise fades into the background. In fact, the whole concept behind Chapters 16 and 17 is based on this idea, and we'll look at it in more detail there.

DON'T GO ROGUE

Revolution can be powerful, but this is probably not the time to go rogue and start disobeying instructions you've been given by subject leads. You may already have the autonomy to unlink your content from your topics, in which case I wholeheartedly recommend you do so at your earliest convenience and see how much time you save and monitor the impact on your class's innovated work.

If not, then it is definitely worth showing this book to the decision-makers in your school (or get them to buy their own copy – you never know, they might not give it back) and ask them to consider allowing you to try it if they aren't fully convinced already.

Other than to impart information, I struggle to find a reason that content should link closely to the topics you are teaching. Instead, I can think of lots of reasons why it shouldn't. It will save you time both in the short term (it's easier to create content if you aren't trying to shoehorn it into a topic) and in the long term when you don't need to rewrite it when your topics change; it will give your class a wider context for each text type; and you will hopefully notice more innovation from them simply because they have to and you might begin to see that they take on board the scaffolding or SPaG links you are writing for when they aren't distracted by relevant topic content as well.

TEACHER TASK 12

This is a good time to dig out the old content that you've been looking at throughout the book and reflect on whether it was linked to a specific topic or not.

The good thing about embracing a life away from topic-linked texts is that it doesn't matter if your older content was linked. Moving forward, if it worked and you know that it's correctly levelled (or can adjust it accordingly), then it will work for any future topics.

That informal postcard you wrote home from the beach for your seaside topic will serve just as well as a postcard or informal letter home when you revisit the text type in your dinosaurs topic, for instance. You've just saved yourself having to write another text and your class will be able to innovate their own dinosaur-themed postcard home (perhaps they've been transported back in time?) without clinging to your model as a crutch.

Look through as many texts as you want to, and see if any of them can be used with your current or future topics if you break the link to your topics.

All of this shows you that you can cut down the time taken to create content and increase the effectiveness of it within your class if you take away the need to link them to your topic.

In the next chapter, we will look further at how you can recycle content that you've already written by thinking creatively about linked text types and by using texts across subjects.

15

RECYCLING — NOT JUST FOR YOUR RUBBISH

Reduce, reuse, recycle. It's not just a handy saying to get people to think about their impact on the environment; it's also a great way to think about the ideas in this chapter. As with the rest of this section, one of the main aims of these activities is to *reduce* the time it takes you to create engaging and impactful content. But how will reusing and recycling achieve this?

If you are spending a lot of your time writing content, isn't it reasonable to expect it to work hard for you? At the minute, you might be spending an hour writing a piece of content to use in a single lesson (though you won't be after reading this book!). That means that your time to work output is an hour per lesson. That's not sustainable.

One of the ways you've learned to reduce this throughout this book is by using the tips and tricks to take less time to write each piece of content. The next step is to find ways to use that piece of content more than once. If you've been able to take my advice in Chapter 14 and step away from insisting every piece of content is topic-linked, this becomes even easier.

REUSE: MAKE YOUR CONTENT WORK HARDER

Reusing your text, in this context, means taking a piece of content that you have created and levelled and using it in another context. It's that simple. When you reuse a text (as opposed to the next section on *recycling* content), you won't be changing it at all. Instead, you'll put it to work again.

In our imaginary world, you've just spent some time writing a brilliant piece of content. You've narrowed down its purpose – to impart information on the Madagascan hissing cockroach – and spent a few minutes making sure that it is at the correct reading level for your class. You hand out copies of the text, your class reads it and take notes, recording your curated information in their own content. Brilliant – it has achieved its purpose. But it doesn't need to be consigned to the bin just yet.

Without touching the text at all, you can give it a second chance. Write some questions to go alongside it, and you've got a reading comprehension activity for a future session or leave it as it is and use it as a scaffolding text for a non-chronological report further down the line.

If you've started by writing a reading comprehension text, you have different choices. If you've focused primarily on retrieval questions, mix it up and use the same text for inference or vocabulary-based questions. Depending on its content, use it as a scaffolding text in an appropriate unit (this is much easier if you don't have to worry about tying it to a topic).

Say your content, written as a reading comprehension exercise, is a letter to a politician bemoaning a local issue. You've used it as a comprehension text, but now you are rightfully demanding more from it. It will naturally have the correct criteria for a formal letter because that's what you wrote it as, so it lends itself easily to becoming a scaffold text for a unit on formal letter writing. Once you've done that, you can then even go on to use the exercises in the recycle section below to get even more use out of it.

One big benefit of recycling texts like this is that the children have already been exposed to it, so any unfamiliar language or complicated text structures will already have been tackled. The second time around, they will be better able to focus on the new purpose and will access it quicker. You will also find that those who struggled slightly the first time around will now access it more easily. While that might not be a good idea if you are using it for a more formal reading comprehension assessment, for any English-based units, it doesn't matter.

When we talked about the purpose of your text, I didn't list 'reading comprehension' as an option. That's because it's a very specific purpose that is hard to get wrong – it's unlikely you will be spending too much time focusing on cramming SPaG objectives or scaffolding points into a reading text. But that doesn't mean that you can't reuse or recycle content that started life as a reading comprehension. It was also a deliberate choice because the purpose of content for an English lesson shouldn't be to test reading comprehension – if the content you are providing is too challenging as a reading comprehension, it's probably going to distract from the primary purpose of the text.

The important thing about reusing your content is that it shouldn't require any changes to the text; we'll cover that in the next part of this chapter. Instead, it's about finding ways to take the content that you've already worked hard to create and make it earn its keep. Don't forget, if you only use it one extra time, then it's halved the time you'd have spent otherwise. If you get a third or fourth use, then a piece of content that took 20 minutes to create is suddenly averaging only 5 minutes per use. That's a time I think we can all get on board with.

RECYCLE: MIX UP YOUR CONTENT TO SAVE TIME

Recycling your texts is another easy and effective way to get the most out of your content. Whereas when we reused our texts, we repurposed them without changing the content, with recycling, we are going to be altering them slightly to give them a new lease of life.

One of the first things that's easy to forget is that there are links between text types when it comes to structure, language and layout. Some, such as a newspaper article, might fall slightly outside of that remit, but they can still link to other text types.

Look at Figure 15.1. This shows the links between several different common text types that you might be creating for your class. It's not intended to be exhaustive, but it gives us a good point to start from.

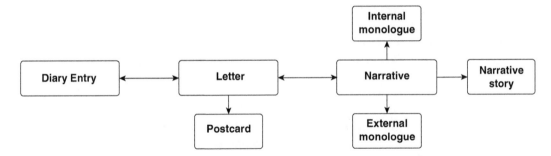

Figure 15.1   The links between several different common test types

For this exercise, we're going to be using the following diary entry, intended for a Year 4 class. The purpose will be to meet a SPaG objective; in this case, the use of formal language in a historical context.

Dear diary,

Today, I boarded the fabulous new ship called the Titanic. *I'd heard how luxurious it was, but I wasn't prepared for the plush carpets, ornate woodwork and vast chandeliers that greeted me when I entered the main dining room.*

I know how lucky I am to be here. Had Father not paid for my ticket, I'd never have been able to indulge my whimsical fantasy of seeing the great continent across the ocean. Perhaps I should remember to bring him back a gift of some sort?

I've already managed to check into my room; there's a marvellously large lounging area and a bed so comfortable that I might never want to leave! I must admit, the artwork on the walls is not to my taste, though I am fascinated to learn how they stay put when the ship begins to rock and roll on the waves.

Ever since I boarded, I've had a rising sense of adventure. Who knows what treasures abound on the other side of the ocean? Will I meet the strange native folk that I've heard so much about? Or will it be filled with the puritans who headed over there so long ago? I wonder what the food tastes like and whether they drink wine like us?

I'm finding that I can barely keep still. We don't set sail (is that the correct term even though we don't have sails? Perhaps I'll have to ask the captain) for another hour or so, and we won't dine until seven this evening. I've heard rumours that there may be ballroom dancing in the hall before that, but I'm travelling alone; it wouldn't be proper for me to dance with strange men.

Anyway, I'm sure I shall find ways to entertain myself. Until then, bon voyage!

Rose

Using the ATOS system, this text has a book level of 3.7, which means that 75 per cent of my hypothetical Year 4 class would be able to access it. Now that I know it's at the right level, I can use it with my class. But that took me 20 minutes to write. I don't want to just use it once and be done with it.

Later on in the year, I know that I'm going to be teaching a unit on writing a formal letter. In your context, it might not be later in the year; you might change units next year and have to cover formal letter writing. It doesn't matter if you recycle a text immediately, within a few months or the next year; the time saving is always there and there isn't a use-by date on written content.

Consider a diary entry. What is it if not a letter to oneself? We can use this link to our advantage and very quickly and easily turn our diary entry into a letter.

Dear **Father**,

Today, I boarded the fabulous new ship called the Titanic. *I'd heard how luxurious it was, but I wasn't prepared for the plush carpets, ornate woodwork and vast chandeliers that greeted me when I entered the main dining room.*

I know how lucky I am to be here. Had **you** *not paid for my ticket, I'd never have been able to indulge my whimsical fantasy of seeing the great continent across the ocean.* **You will never know how grateful I am to you for this, but rest assured that I am.**

I've already managed to check into my room; there's a marvellously large lounging area and a bed so comfortable that I might never want to leave! I must admit, the artwork on the walls is not to my taste, **but you and Mother would adore it**. *I am fascinated to learn how they stay put when the ship begins to rock and roll on the waves.*

Ever since I boarded, I've had a rising sense of adventure. Who knows what treasures abound on the other side of the ocean? Will I meet the strange native folk that I've heard so much about? Or will it be filled with the puritans who headed over there so long ago? I wonder what the food tastes like and whether they drink wine like us?

I'm finding that I can barely keep still. We don't set sail (is that the correct term even though we don't have sails? Perhaps I'll have to ask the captain **unless you know?)** *for another hour or so, and we won't dine until seven this evening. I've heard rumours that there may be ballroom dancing in the hall before that, but I'm travelling alone; it wouldn't be proper for me to dance with strange men.*

Anyway, I'm sure I shall find ways to entertain myself. Until then, **I await your reply**.

Rose

By making the changes in bold, we have turned the diary entry into a letter from Rose to her father. The ATOS book level is still 3.7, so the reading level hasn't shifted at all, and it took less than 5 minutes. Now, I've got two texts for 25 minutes of work – an average of just over 12 minutes each.

It doesn't stop there, though. Perhaps later on in the year, or next year, or whenever, I know we will be looking at monologues. Maybe we'll be looking at the fantastic short film *Little Freak* or using Puck's monologue from *A Midsummer Night's Dream*. Whatever it is, I know I'll need content to teach from.

Some of the key points of a monologue (first-person perspective, include thoughts and ideas, structure it as a thought process) are inherently the same as those in a diary. For my monologue session, then, I might want to focus more on rhetorical questions creating an internal conflict. That will become the purpose of my third iteration of this text.

Today, I boarded the fabulous new ship called the Titanic. *I'd heard how luxurious it was, but I wasn't prepared for the plush carpets, ornate woodwork and vast chandeliers that greeted me when I entered the main dining room.* **Is it too grand, I wonder? Will we be punished for being so boastful?**

I know how lucky I am to be here. Had father not paid for my ticket, I'd never have been able to indulge my whimsical fantasy of seeing the great continent across the ocean. **When I saw the others boarding, those in third class, I realised just how fortunate I am. How have we allowed people to become so poor? I worry that I am part of the problem. Maybe I should offer one of them my room?**

I've already managed to **see my room***; there's a marvellously large lounging area and a bed so comfortable that I might never want to leave! I must admit, the artwork on the walls is not to my taste, though I am fascinated to learn how they stay put when the ship begins to rock and roll on the waves.* **Is it magnets of some sort, perhaps?**

Ever since I boarded, I've had a rising sense of adventure. Who knows what treasures abound on the other side of the ocean? Will I meet the strange native folk that I've heard so much about? Or will it be filled with the puritans who headed over there so long ago? I wonder what the food tastes like and whether they drink wine like we do?

I'm finding that I can barely keep still. We don't set sail (is that the correct term even though we don't have sails? Perhaps I'll have to ask the captain) for another hour or so, and we won't dine until seven this evening. I've heard rumours that there may be ballroom dancing in the hall before that, but I'm travelling alone; it wouldn't be proper for me to dance with strange men. **Then again, is it reasonable to expect me to sit quietly on my own for the entire journey? I think not!**

Anyway, I'm sure I shall find ways to entertain myself.

Once again, the reading level hasn't shifted from 3.7. It's still accessible by 75 per cent of my Year 4 class, and it's now tailored to my specific objective. I haven't had to rewrite whole swathes of it and I haven't had to come up with new ideas or content. It took another five minutes to make these changes, so we're now down to 10 minutes per text on average. If I've made the decision that they don't need to link to my topics, then I can use them again next year, regardless of my topics, and they'll still serve their purpose without any extra workload.

As a final example, we'll look at how the same text can be converted to a straight narrative story. The purpose of this text will be to scaffold describing a setting for a story.

Rose *boarded the fabulous new ship called the* Titanic. **She'd** *heard how luxurious it was,* **but nothing had** *prepared* **her** *for the plush carpets, ornate woodwork and vast chandeliers that greeted* **her** *when* **she** *entered the main dining room.*

A sense of gratitude washed over her. She *knew how lucky* **she was** *to be* **there***. Had* **her** *father not paid for* **her** *ticket,* **she realised she'd** *never have been able to indulge her whimsical fantasy of seeing the great continent across the ocean.* **She made a mental note to take him a present when she returned.**

Before long, she had checked into her room; *there* **was** *a marvellously large lounging area and a bed so comfortable that* **she was worried she'd** *never want to leave!* **Even though** *the artwork on the walls* **was** *not to* **her** *taste,* **she was** *fascinated to* **see whether** *they* **would** *stay put when the ship* **began** *to rock and roll on the waves.*

*Ever since **she'd** boarded, **Rose** had **felt** a rising sense of adventure. Who **knew** what treasures **awaited** on the other side of the ocean? **Would she** meet the native folk that **she'd** heard so much about? Or **would** it be filled with the puritans who **had** headed over there so long ago? **Part of her** wondered what the food **would taste like** and whether they **drank** wine like **she did**.*

*   **She realised that she was** finding **it difficult to keep** still. **She knew that they wouldn't** set sail **(and asked herself whether** that was the correct term even though **the boat didn't** have sails; **she made another note to remember to ask the captain)** for another hour or so, **and that dinner wasn't served** until seven **in the** evening. **There had been** rumours that there may be ballroom dancing in the hall before that, but **she was** travelling alone; **she could only imagine the scandal if she danced with strange men.***

*   **Rose set off to find a way to entertain herself.***

Sure enough, that required a few more changes than the other conversions, but it still only took around 5 minutes. Most of them were simply changing it from first to third person. The reading level has shifted slightly now to 4.0, but that's still within the 75 per cent bracket for my Year 4 class, so I'm more than happy with that. It achieves the purpose of describing the setting and introducing the character and is a scaffold that my class will be able to dissect and innovate from.

For those keeping score, I'm now at around 35 minutes worth of work for four separate pieces of content, which is just under 9 minutes per text – not bad going!

EXPERIMENT WITH NON-FICTION

These adaptations aren't restricted to fiction, either. If you've written a non-fiction text to impart information, can it be altered slightly to become an example information leaflet that your class can use as a scaffold for their own? A newspaper article can very easily be adapted into a narrative with some simple rewording around any quotes. An advert written with the purpose of demonstrating persuasive language can quickly be adapted into a persuasive letter or even a balanced monologue or duologue.

When I've spoken to teachers in the past – and I know it to be true from my own work – the hardest part of creating content is often coming up with the ideas to include in it. When you recycle content that you have already created, that burden is lifted.

When I was rewriting those *Titanic* texts, I didn't have to think about what Rose would see when she entered the ship, or what her room was like, or how she was feeling, or how she'd been able to afford it, and so on. That stuff was already decided from the first text. When I recycled the texts, I only had to think about changing the purpose. You'll notice that I didn't try to remove all the other stuff either; it's fine to leave it in. I didn't spend time removing key diary criteria when converting it to a story; I just adapted what needed adapting.

SUMMARY

It may seem daunting at first to try to find the links between your different text types, but once you start to see how they are all very similar, it can make reusing and recycling your content much easier. This is one of the most effective ways of cutting down the time it takes to create content, and it has real benefits for the children in your class as well.

As we leave this chapter behind us, we are moving on to look at my text vault concept, a system designed to have a broad impact and save time for everybody across the school.

16

THE TEXT VAULT CONCEPT

Did you ever play that game where you had to fill in words in a paragraph to complete a funny story? What if there was a way to use a similar approach to quickly, easily and effectively create content for your class? I'm going to spend the next two chapters introducing a concept that I have called a 'text vault' and showing you how it can be used within your school. The idea is simple enough, but it will take a little bit of work upfront to save huge amounts of time further down the line.

When I first created the concept for this system, I called them 'freezer-bag texts' because the concept revolves around the idea of having a bank of ready-to-edit texts that can be quickly picked up and altered for a class when needed – a bit like that Bolognese sauce you made a year ago and that you have in the freezer ready for when you don't feel like cooking.

Because of the way it works, the text vault system is great for curriculum or academy leads that want reassurance that content being delivered in their schools is always at the correct reading level and does what they need it to do.

I want to preface this whole idea with a strong caveat, though. I love creative writing and I know that a lot of teachers do, too. However, many either don't enjoy it or struggle with the process; this system is designed to help them. Even if you enjoy creating your own content, the text vault system is great to have for when you are in a rush or you just aren't feeling it. It most definitely isn't designed to remove creativity from your work, nor is it the idea to shoehorn everybody into the same structure.

Think of the text vault system as a scaffold that you would give to your children when they are writing. If it's done correctly, then those who struggle will have the support they need from it to succeed. Those who want to fly away and make it their own will still have the freedom to do that.

So, what is it all about?

A SYSTEM BUILT ON TEMPLATES

In Chapter 15, we looked at the fact that many text types were linked and could be reused in a different manner with very little extra work. The text vault system takes that idea one step further and builds up a bank of texts across a school that have already been assessed for their reading level.

As with most of the ideas in this book, the text vault builds on all the other time-saving ideas and, if used together, will further reduce the amount of time it takes for you to create content.

Before we move on to the impact that the text vault can have, let's explore what a template might look like. This is just an example; we'll look in more detail at how you might create and adapt your own text vault in Chapter 17.

> *Dear [diary/mum]*
>
> *You won't believe what happened today. [Main event.] I couldn't believe it when [interesting fact]. [Supporting evidence or consequence.]*
>
> *That wasn't the only thing. Just before that happened. [Second event.] It was like [comparison]. [Supporting evidence or consequence.]*
>
> *Can you believe [rhetorical question]? It made my head spin [replace with other imagery] to even think about it.*
>
> *The best thing is [discuss future event]. That's going to be [emotional language or thought]. Anyway, I'd better be off.*

This is just a short and very bare-bones example of what a template might look like in your text vault. This has an ATOS reading level of Year 2; however, you would expect the texts you end up with to be a year or so higher than that because the content you add will be longer than the placeholder text. We know from Part 2 of this book that sentence length has a big impact on reading level.

WHOLE-SCHOOL OVERVIEW

Imagine if you had templates as those above for every text type in every year group. If you are a curriculum or academy lead, you know that diary writing across the school shows consistent progress because it's embedded into the templates. You know that reading level is being considered and that, even though the template is below the reading age, your staff have been well trained to double-check their final content.

Not only that, if teachers are sticking to the structure in the template, it would be very hard to go considerably over the required reading level. Couple that with any tracking that the teachers are doing of the reading levels for their content, and you've suddenly got a detailed, whole-school overview of the content being created and delivered.

Alongside this, you have a built-in system for ensuring that required success criteria points are being delivered. If you know that all the formal letter templates have the appropriate criteria for that year group built-in, then you know they are being delivered and the progression being demonstrated.

INDIVIDUAL RESPONSIBILITY

This isn't a system designed to become a monitoring tool for leaders, though. If you flip the previous points on their head, as a teacher, you know that the content you are delivering is meeting the expectations of your school leaders. For many teachers, this is an area of concern, so the text vault templates remove that burden.

For those of you who are confident with what you are including in your content, the template I've given above doesn't hold you back. But, as I said at the beginning of this chapter, these text vault templates don't have to be a system that is used every single time.

In Chapter 8, I made the point that the content you are creating doesn't have to be at the exact reading level every single time. The same goes for the text vault. Some teachers will relish having simple-to-use templates that they can drop information into without having to worry about how to create their own content. Some of you will be more than happy creating your own content every time and are using this book as a way to save time doing that.

However, I would argue that even if you are one of the second types of teacher (as I was), there will be times when you've got a parent's evening coming up, three dozen pieces of extended writing to mark, a staff meeting and a school trip to organise. The last thing you want is to have to put together a scaffolding text for a non-chronological report. At those times, you might be grateful that you can just take something off the shelf (after all, we are all happy to reach out online to grab a piece of ready-made content) and quickly adapt it.

Think of these text vault templates as a mid-ground between third-party created content and your own, fully personalised content. You can still modify them to your class's interests and needs, but you don't have to start from scratch. It's similar to the idea of recycling your content from Chapter 15, only you might not have created the original content.

THE TEMPLATES ARE FLEXIBLE

Any templates that you create for your text vault should be designed to be fully flexible across any topic. That way, they only need to be created once and can be adapted as needed. Take the example I gave above. We've discussed the similarities between a diary and a letter in Chapter 15, so this template can work as both.

Dear diary,

I can't believe what happened today. **Germany surrendered. That means the war is over. There's no more fighting, at least for now.** *I couldn't believe it when* **I heard** *the news on the wireless; we'd just turned it on to listen to the news and they were announcing it.* **This definitely means I'll be able to celebrate my birthday in style next month. Maybe my mum will even be able to get some eggs to make a cake.**

That wasn't the only thing. Just before that happened, **Mr Darson knocked on the door with a letter: it was from my dad. He's coming home just as soon as they've mopped up the last enemy soldiers, whatever that means. It was like Christmas, and my birthday came at once. If they can finish their mission soon, he might even be home in time for my birthday. I daren't get my hopes up yet.**

Can you believe **they've actually surrendered?** *It made my head spin,* **and my heart leap** *to even think about it. The best thing is,* **we can start planning a party. That's what Gran said.** *That's going to be* **so exciting. I can't wait.**

Anyway, I'd better be off.

This forms a perfectly good diary entry linked to the Second World War. The added content is, as we predicted, longer than the placeholder text in the template, but the text still comes out with an ATOS level of low Year 3 – it's very similar to the template.

On the other hand, it could become a letter home from the American West if you are studying that as a topic.

Dear my ever-lasting sweetheart,

You won't believe what happened today. **I struck gold! That means I can come home soon. There's no need to stay out here once I've sold it.** *I couldn't believe it when* **I felt it in my sieve; I was just about to pack away for the day when the silt felt heavier. This definitely means I'll be able to celebrate my birthday in style next month. I'm going to try to make it home in time.**

That wasn't the only thing. Just before that happened, **Mr Darson delivered us some good news. There's another wagon train arriving tomorrow with more food; good old fashioned grub from the East.** *It was like* **Christmas, and my birthday came at once. If they can make it here without being hit by bandits, I'll be using some of my gold to eat like a king. I daren't get my hopes up yet.**

Can you believe **I finally found what I came out here for?** *It made my head spin* and **my stomach twist to even think about it.**

The best thing is, **we can start planning a wedding. Think how grand it will be when I return home to my beloved. It's** *going to be* **so exciting. I can't wait to spend my life with you.**

Anyway, I'd better be off.

This one also has a reading level of low Year 3 – it's almost identical to the diary entry. In both cases, the texts fall into the 75 per cent bracket for Year 3. Each one took less than 10 minutes to write and I knew as I was writing them that the reading level would be roughly where I needed it to be because the template was. Not only that, the scaffolding structure is built into it. If that is my purpose for the text, then it's done for me already.

THE CHILDREN WON'T KNOW

When I was putting together the text vault concept, there was a part of me that was thinking, 'but the children will notice that all of my texts are the same, and they'll get bored'. It took me a while to realise that they won't because they won't be seeing every piece of content that I create. Not only that, they will only be identical if I do what I've done in this chapter and use the same template for two pieces.

There is nothing stopping you from creating a couple of diary entry templates and a couple of letter templates. One might be more formal than the other or more or less dramatic.

I wouldn't use this one template for a piece of content in September and then again in May because it's unlikely that I'd be covering the same outcomes. But I might use it again next year for a different topic, in which case the children won't realise because it will be a different class.

IT DOESN'T STOP WITH THE TEMPLATE

I mentioned earlier that the text vault concept sits alongside the other ideas in this book and I think it's important to remember that. Once you've taken a template and adapted it to suit your needs, that shouldn't be the end of it. The ideas of recycling and reusing it that we discussed in Chapter 15 are still completely valid for your new content created from a template.

The templated content that you've built should sit alongside any content that you've created from scratch and be forced to work just as hard for you. I could reuse either the diary entry or the letter home and turn them into reading comprehensions with the addition of some questions, or I could recycle the letter as a diary entry for the husband trapped out West or the diary as a letter a loved one on the front line.

BE FLEXIBLE

I don't own the text vault concept. I haven't trademarked it or stuck a price on it. I firmly believe that it is something that you and your school can take and adapt to meet your own needs. The templates should be flexible enough to support teachers who want a bit of help getting their content created while also allowing those who are more confident to take it where they want to while also knowing that the safety net of pre-levelled and pre-structured scaffolding is there already.

The system itself should be as flexible. Just as I was reluctant to put a definitive figure on exactly how often a text should be levelled spot-on, there is no right answer to how often a teacher should be using a text vault template.

School leaders will know their staff and their individual school's needs. It might be that a school with a strong focus on ensuring consistent progress wants their staff to use them more often, whereas a school that is focusing on reducing workload will give teachers the option to use them when they wish. It should be that flexible.

If I were to step down from this fence for a moment and offer a rough figure, I would probably suggest that templates are used once a half term. That will ensure that every child is exposed to a correctly levelled text at least that often, it will free up teachers' time and it will ensure consistency.

In the next chapter, we will move on to looking at how you can create your own text vault in your school, how you can ensure you maintain creativity and staff autonomy with it, and have a go at creating your own template.

17

BUILDING YOUR OWN TEXT VAULT

If you've decided that the text vault concept is something that will benefit your school, then the next step you need to consider is how that will look in your context. Where you start and how it ends up looking will vary from school to school, but I think the logical place to start is by looking at what you will actually need.

MAPPING OUT THE VAULT

No, it's not a line from a terrible crime-heist thriller, but it's a good way to look at what a text vault will look like within your school. For this, we are going to use the grid in Appendix B. You might have noticed that I haven't included any space for information about topics being taught – remember, the idea of the templates is that they are generic and can be adapted to use for any topic focus. You might want to use a separate copy of the appendix sheet for each group that you are plotting out or create a single document that covers the whole school.

The first thing to decide is who will be using these templates. I've deliberately not labelled the first column as Year group because you might be running this on your own or it might be specific teachers who are using it across the school. You might also have different groups within a class that will have different templates. You might wish to have separate templates for those who need a lot of additional support or you might have different content for children working on different projects. This is the place to really think about who these templates will be created for – add them to the first column.

Along the top, the column headings are equally vague. You might decide to create a template for each half term, in which case you will only need six templates for the year. Others might choose to create a template for each unit taught in each year group and then allow the teachers to decide which one to use each half term. That way, they are always there if they need them at another point. For this reason, each column represents a template rather than a period of time or topic.

Once you've filled in the grid, you will have a full map of how the vault will look in your school. This is also a great opportunity to look at which text types are progressing across the school and where. If there is a gap, you can use this to plug it. This progression will also be important when it comes to creating the templates.

CREATING THE TEMPLATES

Who creates the templates? I'm going to be annoying once again and offer no firm answer! It really depends on your school and the responsibilities within it. It also depends on whether you have staff who are confident creating content and levelling them using the systems mentioned in Part 2.

If you are creating templates for every unit in a typical primary setting, then you might need as many as 72 different templates (based on an average of two three-week units per half term over six year groups). That's a lot to create on your own, especially when we are looking at reducing workload. The other option is to have each year group create their own and add them to the vault. There are pros and cons to each option.

As you can see, it's not a decision that has a right or wrong answer. As a teacher, I would have relished the opportunity to create my own templates, but as a subject lead, I would have wanted to ensure that I had confidence that everything I needed to be included was. This isn't insurmountable and working with peers from other year groups to ensure each

Table 17.1 The pros and cons of your options

One person creates them all	
Pros	**Cons**
Consistent format and structure across the school.	Increased workload for yourself.
You can ensure that they are all meeting the requirements that are expected in each year group to ensure progression.	It will take longer to finish the vault.
Reduces the workload on the rest of the staff considerably.	Some staff will feel as though their autonomy has been removed.
Each person or year group creates their own	
Pros	**Cons**
Each year group can create texts that tie in with their requirements.	You have less control over progression unless you monitor the templates that are created.
Spreads the workload across the school.	You may end up with different formats and styles, which makes it harder for other staff to adapt at a later point.
More autonomy for teachers.	
Staff who lack confidence are encouraged to up-level their skills.	

other's templates work is a great way to encourage conversation and to look at how reading levels change across the school.

When I first started writing reading comprehensions for The Literacy Shed and began levelling them, I was surprised by how hard it was at first to get texts down to a Key Stage 1 level. Equally, it can be surprising how tricky a Year 6 text can be. By encouraging teachers to assess content outside their own year group, you will help to increase their confidence in understanding and writing to specific reading levels.

HOW TO BUILD A TEMPLATE

I think there are two different ways to approach creating a template – either by forward- or reverse-engineering them.

FORWARD ENGINEERING

This is a good way to approach a template if you don't have anything created already or you want to hit specific structural or grammatical elements.

Let's say we are trying to create a template for setting the scene in a narrative. A good way to hook a reader at the beginning is to start with a piece of action, so we are going to create that as the first part of our template.

> *[Character] woke up and opened their eyes. [Describe a dramatic thing that they saw or remembered.] They felt the springs of their mattress poking into their back. [Change to describe what they can currently feel.]*

That gives less-confident staff enough to go on to begin their story, whereas more confident teachers can take it as far as they like. They can even change the *opened their eyes* into another revealing action. It also hits the criteria of beginning to introduce the location to the scene.

We also know that we need to start building the character at this point through characterisation. We can add this as the next paragraph.

> *Even though [describe something that the character is feeling], they [give an opposing action or thought]. They knew it was [dangerous/exciting etc.], but [they just wanted to hide away/run towards it, etc.].*

You can add more to this as you see fit depending on the age of the children it is targeted towards, but it gives enough scaffolding and prompts to begin to build the character within the scene.

By working through the structure of your text type in this way, you can build up a template from scratch quite quickly. This is where the idea of being clear with your purpose (Chapter 13) is also important. Creating a template with a clear purpose will be easier, quicker and more easily adapted than one that is muddled.

If you are clear that the purpose of the template will be to show the structure of a text type, then working through a success criteria list will make it easy. If the purpose will be SPaG objectives, then the order or even occurrence of those structural elements is less important. You can write a diary without internal conflict, and a diary entry template that focuses on the use of varying tenses wouldn't need to include it, so you can ignore it unless it happens naturally.

On the other hand, a diary entry template that focuses on the structural elements probably *would* need to include internal conflict at some point, but wouldn't need to have examples of varying tenses. It wouldn't matter if it was in there – for instance, if you were recycling or reusing a text – but you don't have to spend time trying to force it in.

REVERSE ENGINEERING

You might have already spent some time creating a piece of content that you are happy with. Creating a text vault needn't mean throwing all of that out of the window. Reverse engineering in this context just means taking a piece of content and working backwards to a template.

Consider the following newspaper report with a purpose focused on direct and indirect speech.

Yesterday, just before noon, a violent eruption from the crater of Mount Vesuvius cast a dark shadow over the city of Pompeii. Tonnes of ash and smoke were thrown into the atmosphere and thousands of people descended into scenes of panic.

For the past few months, there had been rumours that something was about to happen. The ancient sage Paulinus had been heard saying that the gods were angry with the people of Pompeii. He pointed out that there have been fewer people visiting him to offer prayers lately and that the people deserved any punishment that Vulcan felt it necessary to inflict upon them.

Even though the ash continues to rain from the sky and has today been joined by noxious gases, many are choosing to stay in their homes. Some are even flooding into the town from the surrounding countryside. 'It's surely got to be safer here in these buildings than out in the open,' Augusta Pollio (23) said when we asked her why she had left her farm behind.

One gentleman, who wished to remain anonymous, said, 'This is nothing compared to the eruptions we used to get. These people today don't know they're born.'

It seems that the eruption is going to continue to impact our lives for the coming days, but this newspaper will be here to report on the facts as they happen.

This has an ATOS level of 4.2, which puts it in the 25 per cent Year 3 or 75 per cent Year 4 level. It includes good examples of direct and reported speech, which were the focus, and so it fulfils its purpose. Now that we have this text, we can reverse engineer it to give us a solid template. All we need to do is remove anything that is linked to the topic of Pompeii and replace them with suggestions for future writers to add.

[Introduce when the event happened; explain what the main event was]. [What was the secondary effect of the incident?]

For the past few months [change timescale accordingly; include information about something that has happened in the build-up or to cause the incident]. [Include an indirect speech quote from somebody that supports this information.]

[Give a story or piece of information that seems to contradict the main event.] [Include a direct speech quote to support this, including a name and age.]

[Include another direct or indirect speech quote to offer an alternative viewpoint on the story.]

[Summarise what has happened and what the reporter expects or hopes to happen in the near future.]

If you or any other teacher picks this up in the future and fills it in to create a newspaper report, you know that it will fulfil its purpose and include direct and indirect speech because it is included in the template. You know that the reading level is going to be roughly Year 4, and you know that the sequencing and structure will support a newspaper report. It would be very hard to use this template and accidentally write a narrative or a non-chronological report, for instance.

This reverse engineering can be done for any content that you have created. As long as you know that it meets its purpose and is appropriately levelled, then it's worth adding it to your vault. The more examples of each text type that you can build up, the more choice you will have in the future and the easier it will be.

TAKE YOUR TIME

You won't build a complete text vault in a week. You won't get it completed over a summer holiday (and why would you want to spend your precious holidays doing even more work?). It might be worth using the advice throughout this book to create content for your class as you approach each unit and then reverse engineer them to add to your vault along the way. It may take you a year to get most of the templates that you need, but that won't matter because you won't need any that you aren't already creating.

Next year, you shouldn't need to create many new templates, so any you do build will just add to the vault as you create them. The whole concept is designed to be organic and flexible, and to save you time, so use that to your advantage and build it as you go along. You might realise that you want to change the style slightly as you progress, which is okay too. It's your vault for your school; all I'm doing is giving you the base to build on.

TEMPLATES DON'T HAVE TO BE EMPTY

The example templates that I've given in this chapter and in Chapter 16 are all what I call 'empty templates'. There is information on what needs to go where, but it's up to the teachers to fill them in. Another option to consider, especially if you have a larger number of teachers who are trying to build their confidence in this area, is to leave the templates pre-filled.

To do this, you could take the example newspaper article and instead of removing the bits that can be altered, just highlight them either in a different colour or with underlining or anything like that. One of the biggest benefits of doing this is that you are showing the content creator (which, don't forget, may not be the template creator) exactly what kind of content you had in mind for each little bit. If a teacher is struggling with creating content, this kind of support can be invaluable to help them realise what it might look like.

While some teachers might see *[what was the secondary effect of the incident?]* and know exactly what you mean, others might draw a blank. If you left in *Tonnes of ash and smoke were thrown into the atmosphere, and thousands of people descended into scenes of panic,* then it is very clear what you mean.

This should definitely be a judgement call from whoever is deciding on the overall vault policies. Pre-filled templates can sometimes seem more restrictive for those teachers who are confident and want to take it further – the best thing to do is to discuss it as a staff and consider people's thoughts on the matter.

CREATIVITY AND AUTONOMY ARE VITAL

One of the main purposes of the text vault concept is to provide a framework for teachers to create effective and impactful content regardless of their level of confidence. If it removes any creativity and autonomy, then it will remove all enjoyment and pride from what is a very creative task. This will only serve to turn teachers off of the process, which is completely counter-productive.

If you build your text vault in a way that encourages those teachers who are more confident to expand and innovate from the templates, then you will soon find that those who are less confident soon become more confident and fly with it as well.

A well-designed template will make it easy and quick to create content that meets a specific purpose, just like the newspaper template did with direct and indirect speech. Because we now know that a single clear and defined purpose is going to lead to better and more effective content, anything else becomes a bonus.

If Teacher A lacks confidence, so they take the template and insert the basic pieces of information and nothing more, their class will have accessed a piece of content at an appropriate reading level that gives a consistent SPaG example in line with the school's expectations.

If Teacher B is feeling more confident and takes the same template and adds more information, just like the original newspaper report that I reverse engineered, then their class will still get access to a piece of content at an appropriate reading level with a consistent SPaG example in line with the school's expectations. The rest is just bonus content that the teacher might use to particularly engage their class or to highlight the use of a particular word class (without making it a purpose of the text).

The point is that both teachers have produced exactly what the class needs from that template, regardless of their confidence and are not hampered by the template itself.

TEACHER TASK 13

You are going to have a go at creating your first template for your own text vault. How you do this is up to you and might depend on where you are in your teaching cycle.

If you are about to create a piece of content for your class, you could start by forward engineering a template based on what your purpose will be for that content.

If you have just created a piece of content, you could reverse engineer it to build a template. Alternatively, you could take one of the pieces of content that you've already created in the past and use that.

However you choose to create it, the important thing is to think about how the template could be used in the future. It should be generic enough to fit any topic but structured enough to make sure that any resulting pieces of content meet the purpose that you are aiming for.

For bonus points, you could take your finished template and try to use it to write a piece of content that is completely different from what you had in mind or what you started with. If you can do that easily enough, then you have a great template on your hands!

Now we've reached the end of the text vault concept, you can hopefully see how it builds on everything else we've covered in the book and can contribute to helping you to save time when creating content. As long as you build your vault to be flexible but supportive, it will have a positive impact.

In Chapter 18, we will look at how you can serialise content to continue that idea of progression across the school and to build characters that the children will fall in love with.

18

SERIALISATION AND ITS IMPACT

The book that arguably made Charles Dickens famous was *The Pickwick Papers*. It wasn't released as a single story, though. It was split up and published in parts between March 1836 and November 1837. It became a phenomenon.

Soap operas such as *Eastenders* and *Coronation Street* have consistently drawn high numbers of viewers for years. Books that are part of a series are more likely to sell well than stand-alone stories. Why is this?

People like to be left wanting more. It's part of our nature to enjoy a cliffhanger; it's why most chapters end on one, particularly in children's fiction. This process of breaking down a story and releasing it in parts, known as serialisation, has been popular since the 1800s. In fact, this type of storytelling is so popular that, at the time of writing, Amazon is currently trialling a new app (Kindle Vella) based entirely on serialised stories.

This is all well and good, but how does it impact you in the classroom?

SERIALISE YOUR CONTENT

That's right: take a leaf out of the publisher's books and continue your content across several pieces. We know that a continuous story keeps a reader's attention for longer because of the reasons given above, so use that to capture the imagination of your class or school.

Whether you serialise content over different year groups or just your own is up to you, but there are significant advantages to doing it either way. As with every other idea in this book, you can use this one on its own, but it works even better and saves even more time if you use it alongside the others. We'll look at how you can adopt it in different ways in a minute, but for now I want to look at how you can make it even more engaging.

BUILD CHARACTERS THAT CHILDREN LOVE

If you heard that a stranger in the street was getting a puppy, you might be moderately curious. If you heard that your colleague or friend was in the same situation, you'd be far more excited. The same is true of the children in your school.

You *could* write a narrative about a character who discovers hidden treasure in their back garden and it might be exciting for your children. It would be even more exciting if that character happened to be the headteacher or other member of staff that they will all recognise.

This is also a great opportunity to engage children with the wider school staff. It's not uncommon for teachers to include themselves in stories, or perhaps even the head, but how often do you include the caretaker, dinner staff or office staff? The children will know them all, and these members of staff can sometimes feel separate from the teaching staff. This is a great way to build a stronger school community as well as better writing.

Include these staff in your stories and watch how the children seek them out to tell them that they've read all about the time they defeated a dragon or rode a camel across the desert. The stories don't have to be true (and unless you have a particularly adventurous staff, won't be), but the children will engage so much quicker with characters that they already know.

That's not to say all of your characters need to be from your school or even real. But the idea of having a recurring character is still of great benefit, especially if you adopt the idea across the whole school.

WHOLE-SCHOOL INVOLVEMENT

Having a running story across the whole school is almost guaranteed to engage your pupils. If they've read a story involving a certain character in Year 1, when they hear they are reading the next part in Year 2, they will be eager to find out what happens next.

A good way to encourage this is to use the text from Year 1 as a reading text in Year 2, just before you introduce them to the next chapter. This will remind them what happened and get them revved up for the next instalment. Not only that, it saves you from having to create another text for that reading session.

You can use this serialised content in two different but equally important ways as you progress through the school. One uses the same text type throughout and has built-in progression but limited scope, the other allows for much more scope across multiple text types but doesn't demonstrate the same progression.

PROGRESSIVE

Let's imagine we have based our character on Mrs Whimsical, the premises officer. All the pupils in the school have seen Mrs Whimsical about and chatted to her, but now it's time to introduce them to her adventures. You want to use a series of narrative texts to show progression in setting a scene from Year 1 to Year 6.

To do this, you might have a series of texts that look like the following:

Year 1: Mrs Whimsical finds a time machine and travels back to the Jurassic period.

Year 2: Mrs Whimsical stows away on a pirate ship.

Year 3: Mrs Whimsical visits the Ancient Egyptians.

Year 4: Mrs Whimsical discovers Stone Age treasure on the school grounds.

Year 5: Mrs Whimsical is chosen by NASA to be the first person on Mars.

Year 6: Mrs Whimsical takes a trip to a Second World War battlefield.

As long as each narrative is engaging, the children will be eager to read the next one. If you tie this in with the text vault concept from Chapter 16, you can further ensure progression across the school within this objective.

By planning the stories in advance and knowing what each year group will cover, you can also ensure that each chapter ends with a cliffhanger leading into the next one. Even though I've advocated not having to link your English content to topics, I've shown here that it can still be done if you choose to.

ADAPTIVE

Using these serialised texts as a way to show progression isn't the only way that they can be used. If you have adopted the text vault system, then you'll have that in place anyway. Instead, you can use your serialised content to explore different text types with the same character.

By implementing the concept in this way, you can keep the children guessing about what the character will be up to next and it frees up the teachers to be more creative with their use of the character. It can still be tied in with the text vault, but teachers will be able to choose which text vault template they use, depending on their class.

In reality, this might look something the following:

Year 1: A fairy tale of what happened when Mrs Whimsical met the handsome prince (based on Cinderella or similar).

Year 2: A newspaper report about a discovery in the school grounds by Mrs Whimsical.

Year 3: An explanation text from Mrs Whimsical about how to use the new sonic toilets that will be installed over the weekend.

Year 4: A persuasive monologue from Mrs Whimsical pleading with the children to clean their shoes before entering the school.

Year 5: A playscript of what happened when Mrs Whimsical met the Queen.

Year 6: A recount from Mrs Whimsical about everything she remembers happening since the Year 6 group joined the school.

If you adopt this approach, you can hit six different text types, all with the extra engagement of a familiar character. There's nothing to say that you have to stop at one text per year, either. However, I would caution against using the same character all the time, otherwise it will lose that spark.

A good approach might be to have one or two real people serialised over the year groups and then a fictional character if you want to use it more than once a year.

GET THE REAL PEOPLE INVOLVED

If you start to base content on real people within your school, you open up a whole new world of interactive literacy possibilities. It will require a little bit of prep work and the willingness of your 'character' (top tip: don't base your stories on somebody who won't be excited about the extra attention), but it's definitely worth it.

This interactive literacy sometimes works best with two different text types, but that doesn't have to mean twice the work. Taking Mrs Whimsical as our muse once again, I might write a letter from the Department of Sewage and Pest Control addressed to Mrs Whimsical. In it, I might detail how a new species of mutant rat has been discovered living in the sewers under the school and that Mrs Whimsical is required to go down there and hunt them.

The text will be purposed as a reading comprehension and the pupils will read it in the morning. Then, at break or lunchtime, I will advise them that they will be writing a newspaper report about the outbreak at the school and they will need to seek out Mrs Whimsical during the break to try to get some information about what happened when she hunted down the rats and to try to get a quote.

Obviously, this will all have been pre-planned with Mrs Whimsical. Depending on how confident your own Mrs Whimsical is, they might need prepping with some information so that they can answer the children's questions, but you'll be surprised how many members of staff are happy to just step into the role and go with it.

It can take a bit of planning and organisation to ensure you aren't encroaching on other people's time, but it's a fantastic way to continue the serialised content that you are using. The children will all come back into the next lesson with lots of information, often different from each other, and be excited to write it up. You could even give them time to compare notes, as in a real newsroom.

If you can't find time for the pupils to seek out Mrs Whimsical, try inviting the 'character' into your classroom for a hot-seating activity. That can lead to any number of pieces of writing and can be a great way to practise note-taking skills as well.

USE FREE RESOURCES

There are plenty of websites out there that offer free royalty-free images that you can utilise to give your imaginary characters a face. This can help your pupils to visualise characters that aren't from the school but that you are serialising across the year groups.

This can also be a good way to add a touch of drama or magic to content involving a real person. You don't even need to get involved with green screens or photo manipulation. Simply stand your real person in front of a whiteboard or projector screen displaying an image (perhaps a tropical rainforest backdrop or the crater of an active volcano); have the person pose suitably and take a picture on a camera or a phone.

CREATE VILLAINS AS WELL AS HEROES

So far, we've talked about Mrs Whimsical as though she is a heroic adventurer rambling off around the world on a series of exciting quests. It doesn't have to be that way.

What if there was somebody else in the school who you wanted to include? There is nothing to stop you from making them the villain. This works especially well if they are outgoing with the children and perhaps a bit larger than life. It also works well if you choose somebody unexpected.

Headteachers are common ground for evil super villains, but the kindly lunchtime supervisor is far more unexpected. Imagine the children's surprise and subsequent enthusiasm when they read about Mr Softly Spoken's evil underground lair, just beneath the grounds of the local newsagents, where he controls an army of three-headed minions. Perhaps he is locked in an endless battle for good and evil (adjusted appropriated for each year group, of course) with Mrs Whimsical.

Assuming you have the engagement of both members of staff, the serialised content could be an ongoing struggle between them, told through a variety of text types. It doesn't need to be anything heavy at all; a Tom and Jerry-style relationship would work well, where one of them is always coming out on top.

BREAK UP A SINGLE STORY

I've included this idea last because it doesn't work well with all text types and tends to work best if you serialise it within a single year group, but if you use it across a single year, it can be very effective.

If you have a narrative that you find your class really connect with, it can be worth serialising it across the rest of the year. This doesn't have to be every week, but dropping the next instalment in once a half term or even once a term can be very effective at keeping up their enthusiasm. Because of the long periods in between, this can be quite dissatisfying if extended across multiple year groups, but within the same year is fine.

Again, it can involve a character from your school or somebody imaginary; it can even be a side shoot from content that is being serialised across the whole school. It can work well with most narrative text types – a series of diary entries, letters or newspaper reports that build upon the same story, adding more information in each subsequent instalment can be extremely effective – but tends not to work so well for non-fiction text types.

TEACHER TASK 14

I want you to take this time to think about a character you could serialise across your school. For this exercise, I'd like you to choose somebody who works within the school and who the children will be familiar with. Once you've completed the task once, feel free to go back and use the same structure to create an imaginary character.

Once you've thought of your 'character', try to write a short paragraph for each of the following headings:

- If you asked the children what this person did in the school, what would they say?
- What (fictional) interesting thing would you like the children to know about this person? (Spies, adventurers and secret agents are all fertile ground here, but things like being a detective or secretly a ghost can also work well, depending on the age group.)
- List three exciting things (fictional or real) that this person likes to do in their spare time.
- How could these things lead to an adventure or something going wrong?

Once you've done this, you have a profile of a character who can start to get into mishaps. Most stories involve something going wrong and having to be overcome, whether they are diaries, narratives, newspaper reports or anything else. By thinking about their pastimes or fun facts, you can quickly turn them into something to write about. Do they like rock climbing? Perhaps they get stuck up a mountain. Do they enjoy watching a sport? Maybe they get pulled on to the pitch when the team is short a player. And so on.

A good idea, especially if you are serialising across the school, is to sit down with the rest of the staff and put together a series of incidents that could befall your character and share them out. You'll be surprised how easily you can come up with silly stories that will have your class laughing out loud or on the edge of their seats.

You can even use incidents that happen within the school and dramatise them if necessary. Be mindful of what you choose and its impact on the children, but most things can be adapted to make a good story (do you remember the time the school ran out of glue sticks and the children had to use slugs to stick down their work?).

Serialisation has engaged readers for over a hundred years – take that idea and run with it in your school. You will see how engaged the pupils are when they recognise characters that appear over and over again, whether they are real or fictional, and the excitement at seeing how a story progresses is very real.

One thing that you should bear in mind is that not all children will realise or understand the fictional elements of your content, especially if you include real characters. You will know your class best, but I would advise that it is always worth approaching these texts with an understanding between you and the pupils that they aren't real, but that they can still be fun to imagine. This way, every child can process and understand the content without it causing distress.

As we draw ever closer to the end of the book, I have one more concept to introduce you to that I believe will save you time and make it easier to create content when you are struggling with ideas. Let's head onwards and dip our toes in the waters of narrative replacement.

19

THE NARRATIVE REPLACEMENT CONCEPT

Have you ever noticed that lots of stories follow a similar pattern? In *Cinderella*, you have a character in a less than ideal situation who is rescued and has an adventure. The same thing happens in *James and the Giant Peach*, *Harry Potter*, *The Hobbit*, and so many more. We can talk about concepts such as the 'hero's journey' and so on, but that's a bit beyond the scope of this book. All we need to know, for now, is that the overall structure of a story is there to be borrowed.

In all honesty, this isn't an outlandish concept. A lot of the teaching that goes on in English lessons, particularly in primary, is predicated on this concept. After all, one of the purposes for writing your own content is to provide a structural scaffold for your class to use and to innovate from.

Narrative replacement is just my fancy way of saying the same thing and pointing out that it's a perfectly valid way to create your own content. It saves time, is perfect if you lack confidence writing creatively or are pushed for time, and is pretty much foolproof.

The process is simple enough and can be used for any text type, which makes it even more powerful. We'll look at how it can be applied to fiction and non-fiction in the next chapter. For now, let's look at what you will need to get started with this concept.

A SIMPLE STORY

There is no point memorising *The Lord of the Rings* and trying to base something on it. It's too complicated and far too long. You need to be aiming for the other end of the spectrum. I always use *Little Red Riding Hood* as an example, but pretty much any fairytale is a great place to start. You'll be surprised at how flexible the structure can be.

BREAK IT DOWN

When you are looking at stories to use, consider that they will need to be broken down into the following sections:

- The aim of the protagonist.
- The location.
- The antagonist.
- The climax of the story (this is the main point of action, not usually the end).

If you can easily identify those components, then there's a good chance that the story will work. For *Little Red Riding Hood*, these would break down as follows:

- Little Red Riding Hood has to deliver food to her grandmother.
- It is set in the forest.
- The antagonist is the Big Bad Wolf.
- The story climaxes with Little Red Riding Hood discovering the wolf in the bed.

REPLACE WITH YOUR OWN CONTENT

The next step is to replace the content with your own. This will vary greatly, depending on your genre, subject or text type. If you're using the text vault concept, then this can just be a case of dropping your own content into the relevant spaces on the template, especially if you already have narrative replacement templates set up.

If not, you just need to make notes for now. By simply changing Little Red Riding Hood into a First World War soldier, the other options become easier. It will be set somewhere relevant to the war, let's say in a trench. The aim will be to deliver not food but a message to somebody in charge. The antagonist might be an enemy soldier and the story climaxes with them meeting in the trench.

Once you've made these replacements, the narrative arc of the story should almost write itself. You know what happens at each point in *Little Red Riding Hood*, so all you have to do is retell the story using your new character, location and aim, etc. If you get to a point where you are stuck, think about what happened next in the original story.

YOU PROBABLY WON'T NEED IT ALL

There are some cases where you might be rewriting the entire story arc, but more often than not, you'll be picking out a section of the story and using that. We'll go into a bit more detail about what this means in the next chapter, but it's important to realise that you are only thinking about the whole story as a way to inform your own part of it. You don't need to utilise all of it.

UNLESS . . .

Of course, if you have adopted the serialised approach from Chapter 18, you might well want to use the entire story split over several different pieces of content and perhaps even different text types (more on this in the next chapter).

I can see myself barrelling towards a situation where I'm explaining everything that I planned to put into the next chapter, so let's take a break here and have a go at a Teacher Task.

TEACHER TASK 15

This one is nice and easy. Using Appendix C, make a list of a handful of stories that you know well enough to use for the narrative replacement process. Make notes of the four sections for each one and begin to think about how they could be adapted for different purposes within your curriculum. You don't need to think about this in any great detail yet because the next chapter will show you just how to implement this, but it's worth thinking about as you put your list together.

This is just an introduction to what narrative replacement is and why it can be an effective way to break that creative barrier when you are generating your own content. In the next chapter, you will see how this can be used to create fiction and non-fiction content, and some ideas for how you can think outside the box to demonstrate more complex concepts.

20

NARRATIVE REPLACEMENT IN YOUR CLASS

Narrative replacement is a quick and creative way to generate content when you are stuck for time or ideas. It works well for both fiction and non-fiction content and across a range of text types. In this chapter, we will look at how it can be applied to whatever you are looking to create and how you can use it to showcase some more complex literary devices.

FICTION OR NON-FICTION?

These titles are a little bit cumbersome when we are talking about creating content for the classroom, but they are the best we have, so it would serve us well to set some ground rules before we head into the chapter.

It's also important to recognise that every single piece of content you create will, ultimately, be a narrative. It will tell a story, whether it is a newspaper report of the sinking of the *Titanic*, a letter from the front line or a straight-up myth. They are all based on and tell a narrative. When I refer to building a narrative with a narrative replacement later on in the chapter, remember that I am talking about whatever narrative you are creating – fiction or non-fiction.

I think there is a general trend in schools towards grouping text types into fiction or non-fiction; a myth would be fiction, whereas an instruction text is classed as non-fiction. Some schools might group fiction under the header of 'narrative'. This falls apart a little bit for me when you ask children to create an instruction text on an entirely made-up construct. Writing instructions on how to brush your teeth is a perfectly reasonable non-fiction text, but does it still qualify as non-fiction if you are asking the children to write instructions on how to give an alien a handshake?

For this reason, I am going to stick to the convention that fiction or non-fiction is decided by the content. There are still grey areas – for example, does a diary entry from the point of view of a Second World War soldier count as non-fiction because it includes real events or as fiction because the child has created the overall text – but it will serve us for the limited purposes of this chapter. It's also the reason why I haven't split the narrative replacement content into separate chapters for fiction and non-fiction – there is just too much crossover.

Remember, this chapter is all about helping you when you are struggling for inspiration or time. There may be some tips that you think are simplistic, but they are all bits and pieces that I have used to help people get past that block. There may be some things that you don't feel you need, but do try to remember them and give them a try next time you are stuck.

Whenever I give examples, I will be using my breakdown of *Little Red Riding Hood* from Chapter 19 as my base narrative. If you haven't read Chapter 19 or have forgotten what it said, I broke down *Little Red Riding Hood* into four sections:

- The aim of the protagonist.
- The location.
- The antagonist.
- The climax of the story (this is the main point of action, not usually the end).

For *Little Red Riding Hood*, these were:

- Little Red Riding Hood has to deliver food to her grandmother.
- It is set in the forest.
- The antagonist is the Big Bad Wolf.
- The story climaxes with Little Red Riding Hood discovering the wolf in the bed.

For this chapter, I haven't included a Teacher Task. Instead, I'd like you to treat the whole chapter as a task and try to make notes about your own narrative as we go along.

DECIDING ON A GENRE

FICTION

When you are creating a fictional piece of writing, it's always a good idea to start out knowing your genre. This will inform so many of your decisions down the line. Often, you'll head into creating content knowing this, but it's always a good idea to spare a few seconds just narrowing it down, much like you do with the purpose of the text.

Some genres can be far too broad to be of any use until you narrow them down. Horror is a good example of this. Sitting down with the intention of writing a scary piece of writing is far too broad. Try to narrow it down to a smaller sub-genre.

Sometimes, it can help to think of it in terms of films. *Scream* is scary because it's filled with gore and takes place in people's homes and schools, an area that should be safe. Films like *The Ring* or *The Exorcist* are scary because it's an unknown, unseen force acting on the characters.

Do you want your story to be claustrophobic with the characters trapped and under attack (Jennifer Killick's book *Crater Lake* is a great example of this and is suitable for Year 6) or more agoraphobic (try watching the brilliant short film *Francis*)? Being hunted by a werewolf that's chasing the character through a forest would be tense and scary, but the language choices would be very different.

Once you've decided on your genre, you can start to think about how this will affect your narrative replacement choices.

NON-FICTION

If you are basing your content on a real event, the genre becomes less important but not unimportant. Retelling the sinking of the *Titanic* could be an incredibly tense piece of thriller writing or it could be a detective mystery where the character tries to work out what is going on in a short space of time. It could be told as a loving letter home, filled with emotion and grief. It's still important to consider the genre, even though the ultimate outcome is decided by historical fact.

AIM

The aim needs to be the driving force behind your narrative. With non-fiction content, this will be largely self-explanatory – escape the *Titanic*, reach the South Pole, inform family back home what life in the trenches is like and so on – but with fiction, you might need to think a little bit harder.

If you are stuck at this point, lean more heavily on your source narrative. In *Little Red Riding Hood*, she has to deliver food to her grandmother. Stick with the theme of delivering something and try to think what your new character might be delivering.

Options might include information, news or medicine, for instance. If you are trying to create a narrative to tie in with an Ancient Egyptian theme, your aim might be for a slave to deliver news to the High Priest. If you are focusing on a magic and mystery theme, it might be to deliver a rare ingredient to a healer in the forest.

Remember, at this point, you are only thinking about what the aim is and perhaps noting it down. It shouldn't take more than a minute or so. No part of this process should be onerous; sometimes, it is best to go with your first idea and see where it takes you rather than labouring over it for a long time.

LOCATION

Again, this should take less than a minute to decide and will largely be determined by your genre or historical information. Writing about Captain Scott trying to reach the South Pole forces your location to be Antarctica. Our story about an Egyptian slave has no option but to be set in the deserts of Ancient Egypt. With most non-fiction units, your location will be decided for you, but that might not be the case when you are creating fiction.

If you are conjuring up your own story, perhaps on the magic and mystery theme, you only need the vague location of a forest or a dungeon, for instance. You don't need to create a whole world with a back story and its own lore. Think back to any film or book that you have seen in a similar genre and borrow a location idea – castle, abandoned theme park, desert island, aboard a ship. The reason that I recommend breaking down a story into these sections is that they are often the points where it's easy to overthink when creating content for your class.

Creating this content isn't a creative writing workshop for you. You've worked hard to narrow down the purpose for your text; don't now spend an hour creating a rich location when you are hoping that your class will recognise and focus on your use of passive voice.

ANTAGONIST

This is an area where you can have some fun. The single role of an antagonist is to stop the protagonist from achieving the aim that you decided at the beginning. In some stories, whether fiction or non-fiction, the antagonist might be decided for you. If you are rewriting a classic myth, you might have no choice who your antagonist is if you wish to stick to the original structure. Similarly, if you are writing something from the point of view of a Mayan sacrifice victim, then the priest carrying out the ceremony might logically be the only antagonist.

Don't be afraid to lean on classic tropes when deciding on your antagonist. Your Egyptian slave journeying across the desert might meet your classic cartoon mummy or the Sphinx. Your wizard's apprentice might encounter a dragon or a rival wizard.

One thing to bear in mind is that your antagonist doesn't have to be a living thing. This is a perfect opportunity to start introducing or really hammer home the effect of things like personification. This can be especially useful when writing non-fiction content.

If you are constructing a narrative around Captain Scott's quest to reach the South Pole, the thing that was stopping him from achieving that was the world around him – the elemental conditions in Antarctica. The same could be said of a soldier in the trenches of the First World War. While the logical antagonist might be an enemy soldier, emotions such as loneliness, fear and even the general discomfort of the surroundings can make incredibly interesting antagonists. They can all serve the purpose of stopping the soldier from delivering a message or going over the top, so can provide that conflict that you need from the antagonist.

Consider how this can then play out in your narrative. In *Little Red Riding Hood*, you might have a sentence such as:

> *The wolf stalked Little Red Riding Hood through the forest. She could sense its presence, almost feel its breath on her neck.*

If we take that and perform our narrative replacement magic for our Captain Scott narrative, we get:

> *The howling wind stalked Captain Scott across the frozen tundra. He could sense its presence, almost feel its icy tendrils gripping his heart.*

You can vary the language more if you like, but you can see how a sentence that you would easily write for a fairy tale suddenly becomes a strong piece of personification in a non-fiction context.

The source narrative is always there for you to lean on when you need it. If you aren't sure what might happen next or what type of language to use, think back to the source and imagine how you would write for that. You'll often find that it can just be a case of swapping a few words and it becomes a completely different sentence (hence, why I call it narrative replacement).

CLIMAX

Often not the ending to your story, but instead, the climax should be the most exciting bit. It is the wolf in the bed, the final battle with the dragon, the last stand against the biting cold of Antarctica.

If you are writing non-fiction, this will be decided for you by real events. If you are creating fiction, don't be afraid to lean on your source narrative again. Little Red Riding Hood discovered the wolf in her grandmother's bed; your Egyptian slave might solve the riddle of the Sphinx or run away. Your wizard's apprentice might battle the dragon or face a showdown with the rival wizard.

All you need to make it an interesting climax is confrontation. Your main character needs to confront the antagonist, whether that's a wolf or the elements. They don't always need to come out on top, either. All you need is the concept because you are then in a position to decide which bit to choose.

CHOOSING WHICH PART TO WRITE

Once you've done this a few times, all of that should only take you a couple of minutes. If you are overthinking it, try to stick with your first idea and run with it. You might be surprised what you end up with.

You should now have a pretty good plan for your narrative broken down into four sections. Each one really only needs to be one or two words because you aren't going to use all of it.

Hopefully, you've come into this knowing which text type you are hoping to create, whether it's a newspaper report, letter or whatever. While you *could* write a newspaper report about the whole of your Ancient Egyptian slave's journey across the desert, it will be much easier and more focused if you concentrate on the journey or the encounter with the Sphinx.

The entirety of Captain Scott's journey to the South Pole would make an interesting read, but not one that could easily be condensed into 500 words while also retaining the purpose of showcasing personification as a SPaG objective. On the other hand, a letter home from Captain Scott in which he discusses how it feels as though the wind has a vendetta against them and how the ice waits outside their tent, desperate to attack, could.

You should know your source narrative well enough that you could drop into it at any point to tell that section; that's why I recommend sticking with simple stories like *Little Red Riding Hood*. That's all you need to do now.

If I set you the task of telling your class the part where Little Red Riding Hood met the wolf on the path through the woods, you could do it. All you need to do for your own narrative replacement exercise is tell that story but swap Little Red Riding Hood for a secret spy, the wolf for an enemy agent and the forest for the back alleys of a major city. The aim of the story might come across in dialogue or thought, but you won't be writing the beginning of the story where the mother tells Little Red Riding Hood to deliver the food.

SUMMARY

A lot of English teaching, particularly in a primary setting, is based on the concept of the pupils in the class using the teacher's content as a scaffold to adapt, innovate and make their own. It's a system that makes the process easier and more accessible, and greatly helps to reduce writer's block.

If, as teachers, we refuse to do the same thing due to a misguided notion that it isn't creative enough or is somehow copying, then we are missing an opportunity to help reduce our workloads and creative burden.

Whenever you create content for your class, its sole job is to achieve the purpose you set out to achieve. It isn't an exercise in creative writing for you (although that doesn't mean that you can't treat it as one if you enjoy that and it isn't overly burdensome for you). The moment you start to worry that it won't be creative or engaging enough, you need to stop and remember why you are writing it.

The more source narratives you know and have in your armoury, the easier it will be to pick and choose ones that will suit what you need to create. *Little Red Riding Hood* is a story about a quest, a simplified *Lord of the Rings*. Something like *Cinderella* is more about being rescued and given a better opportunity, a simplified *Harry Potter*. In *Hansel and Gretel*, the two characters escape the clutches of an evil villain just in time, a simplified *James Bond*.

These thematic webs are woven across every story we read, watch or listen to. Even if you spend a day writing your own creative masterpiece, you will still find that it follows a story arc that has been told before a hundred times. Why not embrace that from the beginning and save yourself some time?

21

SUMMARY

There we have it. In something like 45,000 words, I've managed to distill my thoughts, ideas and general recommendations about a subject that I am incredibly passionate about. I hope that came across and that you have taken something away with you that will be useful.

I started out by saying that there was no contract between us and that I wasn't going to tell you that my ideas were the best and the only way to create content for your classroom. I stand by that. But I would urge you to at least consider the reading levels of the content you create and perhaps use some of the ideas in Part 3 to increase the amount of content you create compared to finding elsewhere.

At some point, I made the point that third-party content definitely has a place in your life. It absolutely has to. There will be times when you don't have the time, patience or desire to create something from scratch. Online resources can be a life-raft in those circumstances. My only counterpoint to this would be the fact that a well-structured text vault serves the same purpose while still giving you all the benefits of your own content – extra engagement, correctly levelled and specific, and uniquely tailored to your needs.

When I first heard about the Lexile® and Renaissance® systems when I began writing for The Literacy Shed, it revolutionised the way I thought about the content in my classroom. I've seen the impact that it can have on children. I hope that you see the same transformations within your own context. If you do, please let me know, either by email at info@mattbeighton.co.uk or Twitter via @mattbeighton. It would be nice to know that I've helped somebody!

Whichever levelling system you choose to use, whether you pay for the Lexile Analyzer or use the free and more accurate Renaissance ATOS system, use it as a tool to inform your own judgement, not as a rigid stick that stifles your creativity and scope for style. Remember that some content doesn't lend itself to the structures that will give you a higher reading level; short sharp sentences still have a place in tense writing.

But, most importantly, remember that the suggestions in this book are just that. They are there to encourage you to think about these things in a different way, but not to hold you to them. The text vault concept is one of my favourite ideas that I think could revolutionise the way progression is demonstrated across a school while saving teachers significant amounts of time. But the way I've described it might not work in your school. You might opt to create templates for Key Stage 2 only or to use it for every piece of content. You might decide that the templates are too restrictive and instead you want broader suggestions that work for your teachers. Whatever works in your setting is the correct way to do it.

I suppose even more importantly than all of that is the fact that writing should be fun. As teachers, we often go out of our way to try to make sure this is true for the children in our classes, but how often do we stop to think about whether it is fun for us? It seems that many teachers don't enjoy writing for their class because they struggle with the creativity, making sure that they include everything they need to or ensuring that it is accessible to everyone in their class.

If this book achieves one thing, I hope it's that it can make writing fun again for you.

APPENDIX A

Date Could be specific or as broad as the week, half-term or term	Title/description e.g. Victorian formal letter	Reading level This could be the exact reading score or your own grading – i.e. low, at or high	Purpose You might want to record the purpose (see Chapter 13)

APPENDIX B

Target group — This might be a year group, a specific group within a year group or a specific teacher.	Template 1 — Record as much information about the text type as you find useful – try to be specific if you can – i.e. **formal** letter, **dramatic** diary entry.	Template 2	Template 3	Template 3	Template 4	Template 5	Template 6

APPENDIX G

Original story i.e. Little Red Riding Hood, Cinderella, etc.	The aim Little Red Riding Hood has to deliver food to her grandmother	The location It is set in the forest	The antagonist The Big Bad Wolf	The climax of the story (this is the main point of action, not usually the end) Little Red Riding Hood discovering the wolf in the bed	Which of your year group units could this story link to? Captain Scott, Ancient Egyptian slave

APPENDIX D

Previous Key Stage 1 Reading Paper 2 SATs readability analysis

Paper: type (fiction, non-fiction, poem)	Flesch-Kincaid grade	UK year group equivalent	Flesch-Kincaid readability	Lexile score	Lexile UK year group	Word count
2017						
Paper 1 – F	6	7	76.8	790	4	240
Paper 2 – NF	4.2	5	87.7	650	4	478
Average	**5.1**	**6**	**82.3**	**720**	**4**	**359**
2018						
Paper 1 – NF	4.9	6	83.4	690	4	425
Paper 2 – P	4.1	5	80.8	620	4	78
Paper 3 – F	4	5	90.3	650	4	300
Average	**4.3**	**5.3**	**84.8**	**653.3**	**4**	**267.7**
2019						
Paper 1 – F	5	6	81.2	640	4	377
Paper 2 – NF	2.9	4	91.7	500	3	498
Average	**4**	**5**	**86.5**	**570**	**3.5**	**437.5**

Previous Key Stage 2 Reading SATs readability analysis

Paper: type (fiction, non-fiction, poem)	Flesch-Kincaid grade	UK year group equivalent	Flesch-Kincaid readability	Lexile score	Lexile UK year group	Word count
2016						
Paper 1 – F	6.2	7	73.6	850	5	383
Paper 2 - F	7.6	8	71.5	1150	8	764
Paper 3 – NF	10	11	57	1120	8	593
Average	**7.9**	**8.7**	**67.4**	**1040**	**7**	**580**

Paper: type (fiction, non-fiction, poem)	Flesch-Kincaid grade	UK year group equivalent	Flesch-Kincaid readability	Lexile score	Lexile UK year group	Word count
2017						
Paper 1 – F	3.4	4	88.1	660	4	597
Paper 2 – NF	7.3	8	67.5	910	6	690
Paper 3 – F	5.2	6	81.6	840	5	601
Average	**5.3**	**6**	**79.1**	**803.3**	**5**	**629.3**
2018						
Paper 1 – NF	7.2	8	68	960	6	557
Paper 2 – P	5.3	6	85.6	880	5	229
Paper 3 – F	5.3	6	81.2	960	6	690
Average	**5.9**	**6.7**	**78.3**	**933.3**	**6**	**492**
2019						
Paper 1 – F	3.1	4	89.5	630	4	604
Paper 2 – NF	9.2	10	58.7	1080	7	604
Paper 3 – F	4.3	5	84.9	830	5	872
Average	**5.5**	**6.3**	**77.7**	**846.7**	**6**	**693.3**

REFERENCES

Clough, P. (2000) 'Analysing style: Readability'. Sheffield University, October. Available at: https://ir.shef. ac.uk/cloughie/papers/readability.pdf (accessed 14 December 2021).

Cowan, N. (2010) 'The magical mystery four: how is working memory capacity limited, and why?', 1 February. Available at: www.ncbi.nlm.nih.gov/pmc/articles/PMC2864034/# (accessed 14 December 2021).

DfE (2014) 'National Curriculum in England: English programmes of study'. Department For Education Statutory Guidance, 16 July. Available at: www.gov.uk/government/publications/national-curriculum-in-england-english-programmes-of-study/national-curriculum-in-england-english-programmes-of-study (accessed 14 December 2021).

DfE (2019) 'Phonics screening check and Key Stage 1 assessment in England, 2019'. Department for Education, 26 September. Available at: https://assets.publishing.service.gov.uk/government/uploads/system/uploads/attachment_data/file/851296/Phonics_screening_check_and_key_stage_1_assessments_in_England_2019.pdf (accessed 14 December 2021).

DfE (2021) 'The Reading Framework'. Department for Education, July. Available at: https://assets. publishing.service.gov.uk/government/uploads/system/uploads/attachment_data/file/1000986/Reading_framework_Teaching_the_foundations_of_literacy_-_July-2021.pdf (accessed 14 December 2021).

Fletcher, J. (2018) 'Zone of Proximal Development (ZPD)', June. Available at: www.sace.sa.edu.au/web/iea/research/assessment-insider/articles/zpd (accessed 3 August 2021).

Gee, J. (2005) 'Good video games and good learning'. Available at: https://academiccolab.org/resources/documents/Good_Learning.pdf (accessed 14 December 2021).

National Literacy Trust (2019) 'Gift of reading: children's book ownership in 2019', 29 November. Available at: https://literacytrust.org.uk/research-services/research-reports/gift-reading-childrens-book-ownership-2019 (accessed 14 December 2021).

NGA/CCSSO (2013) 'Supplemental information for Appendix A of the Common Core State Standards for English Language Arts and Literacy: new research on text complexity'. National Governors Association and Council of Chief State School Officers. Available at: www.corestandards.org/assets/E0813_Appendix_A_New_Research_on_Text_Complexity.pdf (accessed 11 September 2021).

readable.com (n.d.) 'Flesch Reading Ease and the Flesch Kincaid Grade Level'. Available at: https://readable.com/readability/flesch-reading-ease-flesch-kincaid-grade-level (accessed 14 December 2021).

Renaissance (2021) 'ATOS & SATs: The perfect match', blog, 23 August. Available at: www.renlearn. co.uk/renaissance-blog/atos-sats-the-perfect-match (accessed 14 December 2021).

Twinkl (2021) 'Twinkl memberships', 11 August. Available at: www.twinkl.co.uk/premium/individual (accessed 14 December 2021).

Walker, M., Worth, J. and Van den Brande, J. (2019) 'Teacher workload survey 2019'. Department for Education, October. Available at: https://assets.publishing.service.gov.uk/government/uploads/system/uploads/attachment_data/file/855933/teacher_workload_survey_2019_main_report_amended.pdf (accessed 14 December 2021).

INDEX